MW00780551

God's Family Plan

Establishing Generational Blessing

DAVID AND KATHIE BURNETT

First Printing 2019
ISBN: 978-0-578-55298-9

Cover Design:
My Design Firm

CONTENTS

Introduction

Part One
David Burnett
Households, Families, Tribes and Nations

Chapter 1	What Is Family?	1
Chapter 2	Prophetic Encounters	7
Chapter 3	Bet From the Beginning	22
Chapter 4	A Nation and Its Destiny	36
Chapter 5	From Old to New	52
Chapter 6	The Power of Choice!	60
Chapter 7	The Power of Parenting	71
Chapter 8	The Power of Reconciliation	79
Chapter 9	Bless the Children	88

Part Two
Kathie Burnett
Emerging Language, Literacy and Prophecy

Chapter 1	Tools of God's Nurturing Love and Gifts	105
Chapter 2	Tools for Nurturing Parents and Developing Parenting Skills	125
Chapter 3	Tools for Nurturing Language, Literacy and Prophecy	144
Chapter 4	Tools of Nurturing Books and Activities	163
Chapter 5	Final Thoughts about Nurturing	179
Appendix A	Resources for Parent Issues	187
Appendix B	Resources with Information about Childhood Issues	191

Part Three
Author Pages

Our Testimony	199
Prayers of Blessing for the Reader	203
About the Authors	207

INTRODUCTION

Bob Dylan told us back in the 1960s, "The Times They Are A-Changin."[1] Most of us would agree that Bob got it right. The times are truly changing; they haven't stopped changing, and they will continue changing until there is no more time to change.

Relentlessly, change is building upon change. The children of this present age will live as adults in a world that is not only different than the world we know today, but it will be a world in which the momentum and pace of change will accelerate at an astounding, if not alarming, rate. A specific example of this is found in the realm of medicine and medical education.

> It is estimated that the doubling time of medical knowledge in 1950 was 50 years; in 1980, 7 years; and in 2010, 3.5 years. In 2020 it is projected to be 0.2 years—just 73 days. Students who began medical school in the autumn of 2010 will experience approximately three doublings in knowledge by the time they complete the minimum length of training (7 years) needed to practice medicine. Students who graduate in 2020 will experience four doublings in knowledge. What was learned in the first 3 years of medical school will be just 6% of what is known at the end of the decade from 2010 to 2020. Knowledge is expanding

---

[1] © 1963, 1964 by Warner Bros. Inc.; renewed 1991, 1992 by Special Rider Music
http://www.bobdylan.com/songs/times-they-are-changin. Accessed 9/15/2019.

> faster than our ability to assimilate and apply it effectively; and this is as true in education and patient care as it is in research. Clearly, simply adding more material and or time to the curriculum will not be an effective coping strategy—fundamental change has become an imperative.[1]

While the example above focuses on the rate of change in the specific disciplines of medicine, education and research, it is representative of change that is occurring throughout society. It speaks prophetically to the need to change how we prepare both present and future generations for the times and seasons in which they will live. This will require us to dramatically alter many of the currently accepted models and methods of mentoring, teaching, training and parenting.

The following pages describe God's plan for managing change and His strategy for preparing multiple generations for the future. In what we have chosen to describe as "God's Family Plan," the relational structure and strategy that God initially established in His blessing of the household of Adam and Eve on the sixth day of creation is explored (Genesis 1:27-28). Over many generations, the foundational strength and wisdom of God's plan has served to prepare and prosper the households, families and tribes that ultimately became known as the nation of Israel.

In the New Testament, God's Family Plan finds expression in the life of Jesus, the ministry of the apostles and the history of the Early Church. As this plan is observed in operation in both the Old Testament and the New Testament, it may be described as "Lamb dependent" and

---

[1]https://www.ncbi.nlm.nih.gov/pmc/articles/PMC3116346/pdf/tacca12 2000048.pdf. Accessed 9/15/2019. Peter Densen, Md Iowa city, Iowa transactions of The American Clinical And Climatological Association, Vol. 122, 2011 Challenges and Opportunities Facing Medical Education.

"family focused." Nowhere is this more clearly demonstrated than in what may be referred to as "The Passover Paradigm" (Exodus 12:1-32). In the Scriptural account of the Passover, individual households are protected by the blood of a lamb and gathered around the body of a lamb as God's deliverance strategy for the families, the tribes and the nation of Israel. Participating in the blood and body of a lamb brought protection and deliverance to a nation, household by household. This was the inauguration of a season of great transformation for Israel.

In the New Testament, we find that Jesus, the apostles and the Early Church continued to gather with their spiritual households to partake of the emblems of the blood and body of The Passover Lamb, The Lamb who takes away the sin of the world.

God's Family Plan is relational rather than institutional or legalistic. Uncovering the revelation of God's Family Plan is prerequisite to understanding and fulfilling the identity and destiny that was established for each of us in Christ before the foundation of Earth (Ephesians 1:3-6). It is in our recovery and restoration of this ancient foundation that the generations of today and tomorrow will be prepared for the changing times to come.

God has a family plan for each of us (Psalm 68:5-6). For some readers, the thought that God would use family, especially their family, as an instrument of restoration may be troubling. Regardless of the dysfunction, abuse, rejection or abandonment we may associate with our personal family experience, God's Family Plan offers a strategy for redemption and recovery.

Holy Spirit is inviting Christians everywhere to establish the foundation of generational blessing according to the biblical principles of God's family plan.

PART ONE

Households, Families, Tribes and Nations

David Burnett

CHAPTER 1

What Is Family?

With so many descriptions for families and what they do, a basic question must be answered, "What is family?" Family is a familiar term as it relates to our own personal experience and relationships. However, traumatic events and dysfunctional relationships may tend to distort and alter our understanding of family as God intended in the beginning during creation.

The more appropriate question is, "What does God and His Word mean in regard to the word or words we translate as family?"

At this point, it will be helpful to establish the meaning of the Hebrew words that are used to describe family in the Old Testament, family from the beginning. As these words are reviewed, you may observe that they reflect a developmental structure and milestones that appear in a dynamic hierarchal order. These words are not only relationally descriptive, but they flow in a God-ordained sequence that progresses or advances from generation to generation, from glory to glory.

Bet

The foundational family word in Scripture is the word "bayith[1] or bet." Bet is Hebrew for house or household. In application (Joshua 7:14), bet is the household of one man.[2] Bet also has

---

[1] R. Harris-Gleason Archer-Bruce Waltke - Theological wordbook of the Old Testament: Moody Press – 1980, 241.
[2] Ibid, 2442b.

the numerical value of two.[1]

By definition, Adam and Eve were created as the original household, or bet. Bet or household was God's idea, not man's.

In Genesis, chapter 1, the phrase, "God saw that it was good" is used repeatedly to describe His work in creation. However, as Genesis, chapter 2, provides additional detail regarding the creation of mankind, it should be noted that initially there was a "not good" present on the sixth day.

> The Lord God said, "It is not good that man should be alone; I will make him a helper comparable to him."
>
> Genesis 2:18

As perfect as Adam was, the unique creature made in the likeness and image of God, an alone Adam was not enough to fulfill God's design and intent for mankind on planet Earth. Creation could not be complete or good without a household or bet. With the creation of woman, Eve, in Genesis 2:21-22, God's bet on Earth was in place and the sixth day of creation came to completion. It was only when bet or household was in place that God could say that His creation was *very good* (Genesis 1:31).

Why is bet so important? Why did God create a household, bet? I believe Genesis 1:28 provides the answer. I especially like the rendering of this passage in The Voice translation.

> God blessed them and gave them this directive: "Be fruitful and multiply. Populate the earth. I make you trustees of My estate, so care for My creation and rule over the fish of

---

[1]https://www.hebrew4christians.com/Grammar/Unit_One/Aleph-Bet/Bet/bet.html. Accessed 9/15/19.

the sea, the birds of the sky, and every creature
that roams across the earth."

Genesis 1:28, Voice

The following notes that accompany this verse in The Voice
translation also help to explain the context and relational
intent of this passage.

> The crown of God's creation is a new creature,
> a creature that can sound the heartbeat of its
> Creator. That creature, made male and female,
> reflects God's own relational richness. The
> human family is to join God in the ongoing
> work of creation. The earth below and the sky
> above with all their inhabitants are too
> beautiful and too good to be left alone. They
> need the tender care and close attention that
> only God's favored creature can give.
>
> Genesis 1:28, Voice Notes

In this passage, as a point of first order, the purpose of bet or
household is established. Adam and Eve were commissioned
and ordained to:

- **Increase**
  God's intent was that all Adam and Eve would put
  their hands to would prosper. God's will is for
  prosperity to manifest in households.
- **Multiply**
  Bet is the structure required for human reproduction
  and multiplication. God designed the original and its
  fruit to be stewarded within the security and relational
  intimacy of a household.
- **Govern**
  God did not set a religious, institutional, military or
  political structure in authority to rule over creation. He

gave that authority to the household of Adam and Eve.

As the fruit of fulfilling these three purposes, bet was designed and destined to form the foundation and provide support for advancement to the next level relational alignment, the alignment of family or "mishpaha."

Mishpaha

As a natural and extended function of bet, the relationally descriptive Hebrew word is mishpaha. Mishpaha may be translated to family, clan or kindred. A mishpaha is a circle of relatives with strong blood ties[1]. Direct bloodline relatives who dwell in their own separate households would be family. In modern usage, the phrase "extended family" is a family that extends beyond the nuclear family and part of the mishpaha.

The first Scriptural use of mishpaha is found in Genesis 8:19 in reference to the creatures that left the Ark following the Great Flood; it can also be translated as "kinds." Note in Genesis, chapter 7, that the creatures were loaded onto the Ark by bet, by pairs, two by two. But, they came off the Ark in kind or families.

In Scripture, mishpaha first refers to human families in Genesis 10:5 in reference to the growth and development of the bet of Noah after the Great Flood. Again, in Scripture a developmental distinction is between bet and mishpaha, between household and family.

In Genesis 1:28, Adam and Eve were commissioned to conceive, birth and build a very fruitful bet that would developmentally become a large circle of relatives with strong blood ties to their household. In God's kingdom, human relationships are birthed in bet and developed through the stewardship of parenting into mishpaha or family.

---

[1] R. Harris-Gleason Archer-Bruce Waltke - Theological wordbook of the Old Testament: Moody Press – 1980, 2442b.

Mishpaha is not a replacement of bet! Mishpaha or family is a by-product of the multigenerational reproduction and multiplication of each household. From a Scriptural viewpoint, family is intended to provide support, example and guidance to the households, parents and children that are developing within its bloodline. Family should serve to create a favorable, protective atmosphere for the formation and development of new, healthy and whole households.

Through the growth and development of healthy and whole intergenerational and multigenerational relationships, God has called households and families to multiply into a further level of alignment know as "matteh" or "tribe."

Matteh

The next Hebrew family word is matteh, which means branch, rod or tribe.[1] Matteh draws its meaning from the staff that was used by tribal leaders. Matteh first appears in Genesis 38:18 and references the staff of Judah, the leader of the tribe that bears his name. Tribal identity would require a direct bloodline connection with a tribal leader.

After many generations, the bet of Adam and Eve multiplied into families numerous enough to become identifiable as unique tribes. Adam and Eve's strong bloodline descendants reproduced, and the increase produced the sons of Jacob, or Israel, that would form 12 distinct tribes.

God's intent was households would produce families that would grow into tribes. In turn, they would produce an even higher level of alignment; they became a nation. Ultimately, each tribe was assigned boundaries, a specific territory in which to dwell. This structure resembles what we might refer to as a state. In their relational alignment within the inheritance of all of Israel, the tribal states might be referred to as the United States of Israel.

This leads us to the next Hebrew word in the hierarchal structure of family; the Hebrew word, "Goy."

---

[1] Ibid.

5

Goy

Goy means "nation."[1] Goy is first used in Genesis 10:5 to describe the development and divisions of the gentiles after the Great Flood during Noah's time. It is used further in Genesis, chapter 10, to describe the development and divisions of Noah's sons after the flood waters subsided.

The term is used again in Genesis 12:2, as God promised He would make of Abraham a goy, great nation. Ultimately, the 12 tribes of Israel became the nation of Israel.

> I will make you a great nation; I will bless you
> And make your name great; And you shall be a blessing.
>
> Genesis 12:2

In Review

God vested the foundational and fundamental authority for governance, multiplication and increase on planet Earth in Adam and Eve as a bet or household. Over a period of generations, mishpaha or family formed developmentally as a support structure for households. As additional generations of children were born and parented in households, as more and more families formed, the families formed relational alliances and aligned as matteh, or tribes. As households continued to multiply over subsequent generations, even more families were formed, and the tribes grew into a relational confederation known as a goy or nation.

In the chapters that follow, we will explore the relationship, authority, power and relevance of this family structure in God's plan for Israel, Jesus, the Early Church and the Church of the Modern Era.

---

[1] Strong, James. *Strongs Exhaustive Concordance* Grand Rapids, MI: Baker Book House, 1983, H4171.

CHAPTER 2

Prophetic Encounters

My portion of this writing is motivated in part by a series of prophetic encounters. This chapter draws heavily from the interpretation of these encounters that occurred over a period of approximately three years, beginning in early 2016 and extending into the spring of 2019. This chapter provides a description of these encounters, interpretation of their meaning, how they align scripturally and what they have to say about the practical, everyday ministry by the Body of Christ in this modern era.

The Passover Paradigm

I have long understood that the Book of Exodus has much to say as a practical guide for our faith in Jesus and our journey into Christian maturity. However, a few years ago, I began to receive insight regarding what has become known to me as The Passover Paradigm. This revelation pertains to the strategic and foundational role of a household in the deliverance of Israel from captivity in Egypt, development of their covenant identity and pursuit of The Promised Land destiny.

In the Book of Exodus, chapters 5-12, several encounters are recorded between Moses and Pharaoh. Scripture records signs and wonders and plagues that God brought against Egypt in the effort to free His people from the oppression of slavery in that land. However, of the ten plagues that God sent upon Egypt, two are especially meaningful in understanding the high value and importance God places upon the household in His overall plan for mankind and the planet. The plague of darkness and the plague on the firstborn are of notable interest in this discussion.

The Passover Prequel

After God had sent eight mighty, powerful plagues against Egypt, Pharaoh continued to refuse to let God's people go free. God hardened Pharaoh's heart (Exodus 10:20).

A ninth plague would manifest in Egypt in response to Pharaoh's stubbornness. In the initiation of this plague, God instructed Moses to stretch out his hand. As a result, darkness came over Egypt. The NIV Bible describes the darkness that fell on Egypt as a darkness that could be felt (Exodus 10:21). The darkness was so thick that no one could see anyone else or leave his place for three days. Yet all the Israelites had light in the places where they lived (Exodus 10: 23 NIV).

This speaks prophetically to today's darkness.

As a household walking in covenant with the Lord, it may be dark *out there* in this world's system and world order, but in your dwelling in the midst of darkness should be light. Every believer's household and dwelling should be a container of miraculous light, revelation and insight. Every covenant dwelling, every believer's household, should testify to the greatness of our God!

Jesus spoke to them again, saying, "I am the light of the world. He who follows Me shall not walk in darkness, but have the light of life."

John 8:12

Passover, A Lamb for a Household

Following the plague of darkness, the Lord hardened Pharaoh's heart once more (Exodus 10:27). Again, the Lord prepared Israel for the execution of another plague, the tenth and concluding plague, the death of every firstborn in Egypt (Exodus 11:1-5).

> However, God devised a *household* strategy to deliver the firstborn of Israel from the death of this plague. That strategy became known as Passover.

The death angel would be released upon the firstborn of Egypt at midnight on the 15th day of the month, Nisan. Nisan occurs during either March of April using the Roman calendar. However, on the 14th day of the month at twilight, all the households of Israel were to sacrifice a carefully chosen lamb or goat.

> They are to take a lamb or young goat for themselves, according to [the size of] the household of which he is the father, a lamb or young goat for each household. Now if the household is too small for a lamb [to be consumed], let him and his next door neighbor take one according to the number of people according to what each man can eat, you are to divide the lamb.
> Exodus 12:3-4, AMP

Once the lamb was slain, each household was instructed to use the blood to mark the doorpost and lintel of each household as a point of identification. God's instructions were to eat the lamb in haste. They were to eat all the lamb or burn the leftovers. They were to be dressed and ready for departure from Egypt (Exodus 12:6-11).

As death came upon all of the firstborn of man and beast in the land of Egypt, God's plan was to Passover each household with the blood of a lamb on the doorpost and lintel (Exodus 12:12-13). When the plague was set in motion, the firstborn of Egypt, from every walk and station of life and the firstborn of the livestock were struck down (Exodus 12:29-30).

The obvious focus of Passover is the lamb. It was the lamb's blood smeared on the doorposts of the Jewish homes that provided safety from the death angel's fury on that first Passover night (Exodus 12:13). It was the lamb that was the center of the Passover meal that evening. A lamb had to die to save the firstborn of Israel.

> Yet, special notice should be given that deliverance from the plague of death was by household. The instructions were for all of Israel as a whole, but required execution and application by household. The whole nation was delivered by one household at a time.

The memorial celebration of Passover, or Feast of Unleavened Bread, was set in place as an ordinance for the generations to come (Exodus 12:14-17). God intended that Hebrew children would be taught about the Lord of the Passover who passed over the houses of the Israelites as He struck down the Egyptians (Exodus 12:24-28). God reinforced His expectation that Passover would be celebrated throughout the generations… **Forever!** (Exodus 12:24).

The lamb of Passover is a prophetic picture of Messiah, Jesus. In John 1:29, John the Baptist referred to Jesus as *"the Lamb of God who takes away the sin of the world."* In numerous passages in the Book of Revelation, the Apostle John refers to the Lamb as a reference to the resurrected, ascended Jesus. Revelation 5:6 specifically refers to the Lamb as one who appears to have been slain.

The memorial expressed in Passover continues to have importance in the Christian or New Testament era. Jesus celebrated Passover (Matthew 26:1-29; Mark 14:1-26; Luke 2:41, 22:1-20; John 2:23, 13:1-30). The Apostle Paul celebrated Passover (Acts 18:21-22) and encouraged other New Testament believers to celebrate it as well (1 Corinthians 5:7-8). In 1 Corinthians 5:7, Paul specifically refers to Christ as "our Passover."

The cup of wine and the unleavened bread of the Lord's Supper is a memorial or remembrance of the Lamb (1 Corinthians 11:24-26). Even in this modern era, the Feast of the Passover maintains its relevancy in that it is an object lesson, a teaching tool to thoroughly clarify the nature and impact of the deliverance that Jesus provided in His death, burial and resurrection.

Indeed, Scripture portrays the Passover as a type, shadow or remembrance of Jesus (1 Corinthians 5:7). But, there is more to be seen. In this, I have come to see Passover as a paradigm for God's deliverance strategy in this present age:

1. The deliverance of Passover required gathering in households (Exodus 12:3-4).
2. Each household chose a lamb (Exodus 12:3; John 1:9).
3. The blood of the chosen lamb applied to the doorposts promised protection to the household and neighbors who gathered in households (Exodus 12:7, 13, 21-23).
4. Israel was protected from the plague that afflicted Egypt and the nation was delivered household by household because of the blood applied to the doorpost of each household (Exodus 12:26-27).
5. The obedience of the households participating in the Passover brought favor and provision to Israel as a nation (Exodus 12:35-36).

Certainly, God has a people, "a chosen generation, a holy nation, a peculiar people" (1 Peter 2:9). But, household is the unit He has historically used and continues to use as the foundation of His plan for the salvation, deliverance and prosperity of mankind.

> God's best plan for those created in His image is that they partake of the blood and body of The Lamb in a household that is leaven (sin) free and covered by the blood of the Lamb. National deliverance came to all Israel one household at a time. This is a testimony to America and all of the nations of the world. *This is the Passover Paradigm.*

Go small! Go home!

This second insight came in the spring of 2018 when I received the phrase, *Go small! Go home!* As I have sought to prophetically understand this phrase, I have come to see that it contains a revelation of Father's heart toward the "little ones" (children), their parents and households. It is a call to congregational Christianity to reexamine the alignment of leadership, staff, facilities and resources as the Church prepares for the season that is before us and even now upon us, a season that holds the promise of great harvest in the face of advancing opposition and antagonism.

> For who has despised the day of small things
> For these seven rejoice to see
> The plumb line in the hand of Zerubbabel.
> They are the eyes of the Lord,
> Which scan to and fro throughout the whole earth.
>
> Zechariah 4:10

In a global-thinking, big-picture world, values of the small, detailed and incremental are often overlooked or dismissed. Without a doubt, all creation reveals the enormity of God who has created an infinitely vast, awesome universe. Yet, modern science reveals that all creation rests on a foundation that is infinitesimally intricate and detailed. The entire physical structure of the universe is composed of atomic and sub-atomic particles that are too small to be visible to the human eye.

The high point of creation is the design of mankind as a being created in the image and likeness of God (Genesis 1:26). The design is much more than the human mind can imagine (Ephesians 3:20). Think about your own body; a uniquely structured, connected mass of cells of varying shapes, sizes and functions that form the living being known as *you*. Can you imagine that the totality of you was once an embryo in your mother's womb? Can you imagine that even as you are reading this, your ever-developing body beyond the womb is carrying out multiple routines, rhythms and commands that are triggered by chemical secretions requiring a microscope for analysis.

> Your Creator formed you with attention to the most miniscule detail. You were wonderfully made according to God's intricate design (Psalm 139:14).

> Now, try to imagine that the plan for the salvation of mankind required God to act on a cellular level. Many marvel that Jesus became a baby in the manger. But, have you ever imagined Jesus as an embryo in Mary's womb?

Go small! Is an invitation to consider that the mind of Christ is more intricately detailed than just a big-picture, global-thinker. He knows the beginning and the end; He knows every sub-atomic particle in between (Isaiah 46:10; Revelation 22:13). He built the foundation of the universe and all creation, atom-by-atom. He birthed salvation into Earth on an embryonic level.

Salvation to the uttermost means *in every detail*.

Go small! The little ones! The children!

Children may be physically young and immature, but they are an eternal spirit being. In the case of John the Baptist, even the unborn can perceive spiritually (Luke 1:44). God set Jeremiah apart as a prophet in His mother's womb (Jeremiah 1:5).

Have you ever wondered what would happen today if Christian parents began to ask the Lord to fill their unborn children with the Holy Spirit in the womb?

Children are very important to our Heavenly Father. They are a significant part of God's kingdom plan.

In Matthew 18:10, Jesus admonished His disciples to *despise not one of these little ones* (KJV). Among the meanings of the word *despise,* we find *disesteem* and *think little or nothing of.*[1] Jesus did not have a dismissive attitude toward children. Jesus said, "Let the little children come to Me; do not get in their way. For the kingdom of heaven belongs to children like these" (Matthew 19:5, Voice).

As believers in this season, a multi-generational call is inviting us to develop a godly appreciation for children. But, what does this mean? We often hear the phrase, "I appreciate you." Most often that is interpreted to mean that I "like" or "value" you as a person. Certainly, from a biblical point of view, God wants us to like and value children.

Jesus truly loves the little children. If we want to be like Jesus in every dimension of our being... If we want to nearer to His heart, we must turn our heart toward children (Malachi 4:6).

According to Matthew 18:5 in The Voice translation, one of the ways to welcome the presence of Jesus is to welcome children.

---

[1] Strong, James. *Strongs Exhaustive Concordance* Grand Rapids, MI: Baker Book House, 1983, G2706.

But, the word appreciate has another meaning. It can also mean, "to increase in value." Our homes, real estate and other investments can appreciate or increase in value if we steward them correctly. It is in keeping with this understanding of the term "appreciate" that we need to learn to appreciate children. Our mission as His children should be to add value to the little ones, the emerging ones.

Go home!

For children, appreciation should begin at home. The foundation for relational wholeness with both God and people has its foundation in the home. God's intent is that children find added Scriptural and spiritual value in our homes (Deuteronomy 6:6-7, Ephesians 6:4).

In this season, it is good to teach children and minister to them in a congregational, Sunday School or Children's Church setting; but, God is calling us to rediscover and rebuild an ancient foundation for more effectively adding value to children. The call is to a multi-generational rededication to "household or family church." It is a call to teach and mentor parents in how to minister to and worship with their children as a household unit in their home.

Children are best served when they receive loving nurture, teaching and relational discipline from parents in the home (Ephesians 6:4). Again, children are spiritual beings from conception (Psalm 22:10, 71:6, 139:13, Luke 1:15). What better time is there for children to be led into a personal relationship with Jesus as their Savior than when they are young? Who better to lead them into a warm, loving relationship with Jesus than their nurturing, loving parents? Who better to discern and develop a child's spiritual gifts than those who know that child best, the child's parents?

> What better place is there than the home for children to see ministry in action, and to experience the manifestation of spiritual gifts, signs, wonders and miracles? Where better to

ask questions, begin their own spiritual practice, make mistakes and receive correction than in the safety and security of their home in the relational, loving care and discipline of parents?

Encounter No. 3: An Emerging Greater Glory Generation
More recently, on December 8, 2018, I received a vision of a train emerging from darkness with bright lights illuminating the rails before it. As I have meditated on the meaning of this vision, I have come to see that it is linked with the previous prophetic encounters.

I have come to understand this vision as insight into an Emerging Greater Glory Generation, a revelation of a new, powerful generational alignment that God is forming among those called according to His purpose. This vision contains prophetic insight for the ministry assignment of every generation of believer, young and old, regardless of age.

This vision is a representation of the church advancing powerfully out of the darkness of religion and secularism, guided by a piercing light. One generation has prepared the right of way and laid the track to run on. The next generation takes up the light and moves it forward in ever-increasing glory, as in the days of Elijah and Elisha. As they move in the light of His glory, many generations are powerfully connected and aligned to assume the weight of a greater glory and the harvest it produces.

> According to Genesis 1:28 God's intent for mankind from the beginning has been increase and advancement.

> We all, with unveiled face, beholding as in a mirror the glory of the Lord, are being transformed into the same image from glory to glory, just as by the Spirit of the Lord.
> 2 Corinthians 3:18

In this era, when we think of the next emerging generation, many of us may tend to think of the Millennial Generation, However, what I see emerging are the young ones, the Post-Millennial generations, even the ones yet unborn. In the manner that God encouraged Abram (Genesis 15:5), God is encouraging us to look into the heavens and believe for the generations and nations that will be born by faith. Your children, or the children you minister to, as well as their present and/or future offspring are soil for the seeds of the Word to produce a chosen people, a royal priesthood, a holy nation, God's special possession (1 Peter 2:9), a ***Greater Glory Generation.***

My faith is reaching out for the children, the little ones and even the unborn as an Esther Generation. They are ones who "have come into the kingdom for such a time as this" (Esther 4:14). My reference to an Esther Generation is not in a gender sense, but in the sense of kingdom purpose, anointing and favor for their appointed season as a generation of deliverance and transformation.

Preparing Parents to Parent
Scripture plainly teaches that the foundational responsibility to teach the children, for spiritual stewardship and development of the next generation, lies with their parents (Deuteronomy 6:7; 11:19-21). One of Abraham's covenant responsibilities was to teach his children (Genesis 18:19). For a greater glory generation to emerge, it will require preparing parents to disciple the children. Training parents and supporting them is a pressing necessity as they assume accountability as the primary frontline minsters to their children.

Our congregations are filled with people who were raised in dysfunctional homes. Not all Christians who are parents have the knowledge, skill or support to effectively minister to their children. Many born-again, Spirit-filled believers simply do not know how to be Christian parents.

Just as Esther's kinsman, Mordecai (Esther 2:5-7),

assumed parental stewardship of the orphan Esther, this next generation will need spiritual "Mordecais" who assume a parental role in preparing them for their righteous purpose and destiny. Some of this next generation will be stewarded by their natural parents. Others will be stewarded by spiritual parents with a Mordecai calling and anointing, an anointing to care for those who would otherwise become spiritual orphans.

If we truly believe that the glory of the latter house is greater than the glory of the former house (Haggai 2:9), we need to humbly and repentantly examine the commitment and value we extend to the little ones and the generations to come. If we understand that God intends for His children to walk in ever-increasing glory (2 Corinthians 3:18), we need to turn our hearts toward the children (Malachi 4:6) and prepare the coming generations to walk in the greater glory.

I believe that it is time to prepare a generation to enter into the glorious manifestation of the greater works promised in John 14:12. If we will accept the call to truly value and appreciate the emerging generation, we will see a manifestation of God's glory as never seen before on Planet Earth.

Encounter No. 4: Setting the Solitary in Households

> God sets the solitary in families;
> He brings out those who are bound into
>   prosperity;
> But the rebellious dwell in a dry land.
>
> Psalm 68:6

God Sets the Solitary in Families

To some, this is a Scriptural promise. To some, this is a prophetic decree of faith. Even though this may not be the present reality of many in the Body of Christ, it is a promise as real and sure as the promise of Canaan was to Israel while in the captivity of Egypt.

God's plan for Israel was demonstrated in the deliverance of Passover, the giving of the Law at Pentecost,

18

Israel's alignment around the Tabernacle in the wilderness and the assignment of the territories in the land of promise. God was moving them forward by each household, each family and each tribe to become a mighty nation.

God heard Israel's cry in Egypt, but He did not just zap them into their destiny. It was a lengthy step-by-step process; a process made more burdensome and lengthy by Israel's disobedience, rebellion and their lack of faith and trust in God.

Aloneness is not God's ultimate best will for our lives. His ultimate destiny is to set us in relationships with people of similar precious faith. Godly relationship takes faith, courage, effort and grace.

> Every Promised Land will have at least a few giants in it. Giants are a hindrance and an obstacle, but not denial or defeat to a people who walk in faith and patience.

Single Does Not Mean Solitary

In 1 Kings, chapter 17, God led the Prophet Elijah to a solitary place of provision for a season, but God did not leave Elijah there. Elijah was sent to the household of a widow in Zarephath. In this household, the prophet, the widow and her son found provision during a season of famine. God also manifested the anointing to heal in this household (1 Kings 17:17-24). This was not necessarily a traditional household or family, but God divinely set the prophet in a household alignment during a season of famine, a season of judgment in the land.

Jesus didn't marry during His earthly ministry, but God set Jesus in a family, or household, of Joseph and Mary. Later, as an adult, Jesus revealed that He had been set in a new household alignment with "whoever does the will of My Father in Heaven…" (Matthew 12:46-50). By faith, we can all become members set in His household.

This might be a good time to read all of 1 Corinthians,

chapter 7. The Apostle Paul, unmarried by his own account (1 Corinthians 7:8), would not consider himself as isolated or solitary. In the Spirit, Paul was a father to Timothy (1 Timothy 1:2). Paul was a father to the Church at Corinth (1 Corinthians 4:14-15).

In the Book of Acts, we find Paul did not travel or minister alone. He was set in alignment with Barnabas (Acts 13:2). Later ministry companions included Silas (Acts 15:40), John Mark and Luke (2 Timothy 4:11), to mention a few.

Just because a believer is single does not prohibit or void the potential for real, vital and miracle working relationships with spiritual brothers, sisters, sons and daughters.

Anyone experiencing periods of isolation and solitude should seek Father's heart for insight into the cause and purpose of this situation. The isolation you see as a punishment may be a season of preparation. Sometimes, solitude and isolation are a prelude to unparalleled revelation (the Apostle John on the Isle of Patmos, Revelation 1:9-19), a new season of miraculous provision and relationship (the Prophet Elijah, 1 Kings 17:1-15), a time before ultimate victory (Jesus on the cross, Matthew 27:46).

Whatever the cause or circumstance of your isolation, God is able to turn it around. What satan has intended for evil; God is able to turn to good (Genesis 50:20). Give Him your heart and watch Him turn it around (Jeremiah 29:11; Romans 8:28). It may not be the way you imagined or in the timing you planned, but with faith in God and His Word, and with the spiritual fruit of patience (Galatians 5:22, AMP) He will fulfill His promise.

God makes a home for the lonely.
Psalm 68:6, AMP

Restoring an Ancient Foundation
As I have searched the Scriptures and sought understanding regarding the prophetic meaning and practical implications of

each of these prophetic encounters, I have come to understand that God is recovering and restoring an ancient foundational operating strategy for implementation in the Church of this modern age. The recovery of this strategy is necessary to realign those called according to His purpose with their original destiny and purpose as described in Genesis 1:28. The restoration of this ancient foundational strategy is vital to the recovery of the identity, authority, power and effectiveness that once characterized the patriarchs, ancient Israel, the ministry of Jesus, His disciples and the Early Church.

> The common theme that runs through the revelation of each of these prophetic insights is the strategic restoration of the relational structure, function and destiny of family in its most basic and practical form.

"Bet" From the Beginning: In the next chapter, we will see how God used *bet* or *household* as a powerful instrument of His purpose in the Book of Genesis.

CHAPTER 3

Bet From the Beginning – The Ancient Foundation

Those from among you shall build the old waste places;
You shall raise up the foundations of many generations;
And you shall be called the Repairer of the Breach,
The Restorer of Streets to Dwell In.

Isaiah 58:12

The perfection of creation that is described in the first two chapters of Genesis became the subject of a clandestine, satanic attack in Genesis, chapter 3. The ultimate purpose of this attack was to separate bet from relationship with God and to steal Adam and Eve's household blessing of fruitfulness, multiplication and dominion (Genesis 1:28). Tragically, the household of Adam and Eve succumbed to the deceitful, cunning schemes of the evil one. They both, as a household, disobeyed God (Genesis 2:15-17; 3:6). Adam and Eve sinned.

In their disobedience to God, Adam and Eve opened the door to disease, death, destruction and dysfunction to the entire human race. What God had blessed was placed under the curse of sin (Genesis 3:7-24).

One of the key lessons of the Book of Genesis is that what begins in bet, or the household, has the ability to ultimately impact the entire world.

Over a period of many generations, for more than thousands of years, the wickedness of sin so infected the human race that God repented of ever-creating man. This wickedness was so pervasive that God decided to destroy all of mankind and all animals on the face of Earth (Genesis 6:5-7).

Household Restoration

> Noah found grace in the eyes of the Lord.
> Genesis 6:8

But Noah found grace. When sin was abounding everywhere on Earth, grace found a home in the household of Noah. Noah was a just, blameless, righteous man who walked with God (Genesis 6:9).

God spoke to Noah (Genesis 6:13). God gave Noah a warning of the coming destruction of all things (Genesis 6:13-17). But God also gave Noah plans for the Ark, a means of preserving his wife, his three sons and his son's wives; along with a pair of all living creatures.

> God chose the bet, the household of Noah, to save mankind and all living creatures from complete annihilation.
> Genesis 6:18-19

The day came when God commanded Noah and his house, bet, to enter the Ark. At age 600, Noah and his household were safely in the Ark as the floodwaters covered Earth (Genesis 7:6). After many days, the Great Flood ended and Earth was ready for habitation. Following a year of life aboard the Ark, Noah heard God speak the command for his household and all creatures to go out of the Ark. (Genesis 8:13-17).

With the floodwaters behind them and in an atmosphere of worship and sacrifice, a divine interchange unfolded. In this, there is a noticeable similarity to God's words to Adam and Eve in Genesis 1:28. God blessed Noah and his sons, and said to them: "Be fruitful and multiply, and fill the earth" (Genesis 9:1).

God extended covenant to Noah and his descendants (Genesis 9:9) and with "every living creature of all flesh" (Genesis 9:15). As a sign of covenant, God set His rainbow in the sky (Genesis 9:13) as His promise to never again destroy all flesh (Genesis 9:16-17).

A Household of Difference

One righteous household can make a world of difference. In the narrative of Adam and Eve's sin, the disobedience of one household spread death and wickedness to all mankind. However, in the Scriptural narrative of Noah and the Ark, notice the significance and authority of one obedient household to impact the future of all mankind for good; to preserve righteousness on Earth.

> Again, what happens in the household doesn't just stay in the household. What happens in the household can impact the world!

> If you are Christ's, then you are Abraham's seed, and heirs according to the promise.
> Galatians 3:29

Beyond the account of the Great Flood and the life of Noah and his sons, Genesis, chapter 10, introduces us to one of the most significant households in all Scripture. The story of Abram, who became Abraham, and Sarai, who became Sarah, is the story of a household that multiplied by faith and against all odds (Romans 4:16-20; Hebrews 11:11-12). It is in this household, God established a covenant that would produce a great nation (Genesis 17:6). As modern era disciples of Jesus, we walk in the blessing and favor of God's covenant promises to Abraham (Genesis 17:1-21; Galatians 3:29).

Once more it is evident that God's calling and blessing on Abraham's household is similar in scope and intent to the blessing of Adam and Eve (Genesis 1:28) and the blessing of Noah (Genesis 9:1-3).

This is more than the recorded history of one man; this is the story of God's plan to reaffirm his bet strategy on Earth. It is a story of real, raw humans as they press through their life's journey contending for family. It is the story of experiencing favor and blessing through process.

A dominant theme of this sequence of events is the battle of bet to press through the discouragement of delay. Abraham was already an old man when he heard God's voice decree his blessing and destiny (Genesis 12:1-4). In the realm of normal physical reality, this is a time-sensitive promise.

In spite of discouragement and delay, Abraham became the Father of Faith (Romans 4:11-12). In Genesis, chapter 15, God reaffirmed His promise to multiply Abraham's household and promised him a son (vs.4). Abraham believed God's promise. According to Genesis 15:4-6, it was in believing in the Lord regarding the promise of a son, a household promise, that Abraham was made righteous.

As with many of us today, Abraham had faith, but that did not stop him from trying to speed up the process of the promise. Approximately ten years after God had made the original promise of multiplication, Abraham and Sarah remained childless (Genesis 16:1-3).

Sarah devised her plan for Abram to have a child by her servant Hagar. The plan worked; sort of. Although this plan produced an heir, it was not the heir God intended. God's covenantal plan required that Abraham's heir would be born by Sarah (Genesis 17:15-17).

> God reserves the right to choose whom He
> will bless as we align as a household. It is God
> who sets the solitary in families, bet.
>
> Psalms 68:6

Covenant Laughter

God appeared to Abraham and clearly stated that Sarah would bear him a son. Abraham literally fell on the floor laughing (Genesis 17:15-17) at the idea that a 100-year-old man and a 90-year-old woman could conceive and birth a child.

Later, the Lord's messengers passed by Abraham's tent on their way toward Sodom. Abraham invited them to stop to have their feet washed and some refreshment to eat. As they visited with Abraham, one messenger prophesied that Sarah would birth a child within the next year. Sarah overheard this prophesy and "laughed within herself" (Genesis 18:12). But, the laughter of both Abraham and Sarah did not void God's plan. As the Lord's messengers had prophesied, Sarah birthed a child (Genesis 21: 1-7). The child was named Isaac (Genesis 21:3), meaning laughter.[1]

Abraham laughed, Sarah laughed and the miracle of laughter was conceived and birthed into their bet. After nearly 25 years of waiting (Genesis 21:1-5), laughter entered the relationship between God, Abraham and Sarah. In essence, God's promise to Abraham was that He would establish covenant with laughter (Genesis 17:21).

From the beginning, God's plan was that the sound of children laughing, discovering and growing would be heard in households around the world. God choosing to make covenant with laughter is not an incidental act or by coincidence. God purposefully named the child Laughter and pledged His covenant to the child. God loves laughter! God's favor rests on laughter. It is apparent in the narrative of

---

[1] Strong, James. *Strongs Exhaustive Concordance* Grand Rapids, MI: Baker Book House, 1983, H3227.

Abraham, Sarah and Isaac that one of the things God wanted to be permanently established on Earth is the bloodline of laughter. If you are a child of God, laughter is in your Spiritual DNA.

Bloodline Intercession

The narrative of Abraham, Sarah and the promise of Isaac is interrupted with an amazing example of bloodline intercession. Lot, Abraham's nephew, had chosen to dwell in Sodom (Genesis 14:12). Because of Abraham's covenant relationship with God and his bloodline relationship with the household of Lot, Abraham's heavenly visitors were compelled to reveal God's judgment against the wickedness of Sodom (Genesis 18:16-33).

The sin of the territory where our bloodline resides will impact their destiny. Abraham's faith relationship with God gave him intercessory authority for his bloodline. We are authorized to intercede for the sinful and foolish in our bloodline (Genesis 18:20-33).

Since Lot lived in Sodom, Abraham was compelled to intercede before God for the preservation of this sin-infested city. In the end, God agreed to spare Sodom if as few as ten righteous persons could be found there.

Genesis 19:1-29 records the story of the judgment of Sodom. Even though ten righteous persons were not found there, God remembered Abraham and delivered Lot out of the destruction (Genesis 19:29).

> As believers, you and I have the authority and obligation to intercede for the salvation and deliverance of our household and bloodline relatives. If we are indeed "Abraham's seed," (Galatians 3:29), we will do what Abraham did (John 8:39). We will intercede on behalf of our bloodline as Abraham interceded. Our faith intercession on their behalf can be a matter of life and death.

Isaac – A New Generation of Blessing

In Isaac, the bloodline and blessing of Abraham was transmitted into a new generation (Genesis 17:19). The word generation, or generations, may carry two different concepts of meaning. The word generations in Hebrew is "toledot," meaning "what is produced or brought into being by someone."[1] The word generation can be commonly understood as "the circle of a man's life," or "a period or age of time."[2] In one sense, the blessing that God produced or brought into being in Abraham's life was transmitted into the life of Isaac. In another sense, the circle of Isaac's life, conception to death, marked a new age, or period of time.

The age of blessing has not passed. God did not intend for the blessing to end with either Abraham or Isaac. God's intent is that His blessing would find rest upon every generation by faith. As with Abraham and Sarah, God's intent is the blessing will be transmitted into the next generation by household, or bet.

Isaac and Rebecca – Continuing the Bet of Blessing

Genesis, chapter 24, records the events surrounding the selection of a wife for Isaac. God's will for Isaac was that he and a young woman named Rebekah would become man and wife and form a new bet. Genesis 24:15-16 records that Rebekah was born into the bloodline of Abraham's brother Nahor and that she was a very beautiful virgin. At age 40, Isaac took Rebekah to be his wife (Genesis 25:20).

Following a period of barrenness that lasted approximately 20 years (Genesis 25:26), Isaac pleaded to the Lord for Rebekah and the Lord answered Isaac's prayer (Genesis 25:21-26). Rebekah conceived twins, Jacob and Esau. Rebekah received revelation from the Lord concerning the

---

[1] R. Harris-Gleason Archer-Bruce Waltke - Theological wordbook of the Old Testament: Moody Press – 1980, 867g.
[2] Ibid, 418b.

future of twins in her womb.

> The Lord said to her:
> "Two nations are in your womb,
> Two peoples shall be separated from your
>   body;
> One people shall be stronger than the other,
> And the older shall serve the younger."
>
> Genesis 25:23

The firstborn of the twins was Esau, meaning hairy. The second twin was named Jacob, meaning heal grabber.[1]

Jacob – Bet to Tribe

In Jacob, we see the process of generational blessing and multiplication demonstrated. The household of Jacob increases and multiplies from bet to matteh, from household to tribe.

Much of Jacob's story is about a man on the run from his brother Esau. Jacob connived and deceived his way into obtaining both Esau's birthright and their father's blessing (Genesis 25: 35-45). But Jacob was more than a man on the run. Before Jacob left home, his father instructed him to find a wife among the daughters of Rebekah's brother Laban in Paddan Aram. Isaac sent Jacob on a mission to form a bet (Genesis 28:1-4).

On his journey, Jacob came to a place that he would name Bethel, or house of God.[2] At Bethel, God talked to Jacob for the first time. Jacob dreamed about a ladder that extended from Heaven to Earth with angels ascending and descending. In the dream the Lord stood above the ladder and spoke blessings over Jacob. The Lord promised to give Jacob

---

[1] *Beacon Bible commentary* (1st ed., Vol. 1). (1964). Kansas City, MO: Beacon Hill Press, p101.

[2] Strong, James. *Strongs Exhaustive Concordance* Grand Rapids, MI: Baker Book House, 1983, H1008.

the land on which he was laying, and that Jacob would have descendants as numerous as the dust of Earth; and that all of Earth's families, mishpaha or a circle of relatives with close blood ties[1] would be blessed along with Jacob and his descendants (Genesis 28:10-14). The Lord promised to be with Jacob wherever he would go, keep him, bring him back to the land and fulfill His promise (Genesis 28:15). At Bethel, God agreed to extend the covenant blessing promised to Abraham and his descendants to Jacob and Jacob's descendants.

Jacob then completed his journey to his Uncle Laban's household in Paddan Aram (Genesis 29:13). Jacob served his Uncle Laban for 20 years (Genesis 31:41). During his 20-year sojourn in Paddan Aram, God blessed Jacob and caused him to multiply and prosper (Genesis 30:43). Jacob labored seven years for the promise of Laban's daughter Rachel to become his wife. However, Laban tricked Jacob and gave him his older daughter Leah, and her handmaid Zilpah instead. So, Jacob labored seven more years for the right to marry Rachel (Genesis 29:15-30). Thus, Jacob, his two wives and their handmaids became a household, bet, in Paddan Aram.

Despite the fact that Laban changed Jacob's wages ten times during his 20 years of labor (Genesis 31:41), God blessed Jacob and caused his bet to multiply and prosper. In Paddan Aram, Jacob became a husband and the father of 11 sons and a daughter (Genesis 29:31-35; 30:1-24). He possessed large flocks, servants, camels and donkeys (Genesis 30:43).

However, the day came when the Lord once again appeared to Jacob in a dream, as He had at Bethel. In this dream, the God of Bethel instructed Jacob to return to the land of his family (Genesis 31:10-13). Without notifying Laban, Jacob departed Paddan Aram for the land of Canaan with his household, flocks and possessions (Genesis 31:17-21).

---

[1] R. Harris-Gleason Archer-Bruce Waltke - Theological wordbook of the Old Testament, Moody Press – 1980, 2442b.

Upon learning about Jacob's departure, Laban pursued and overtook Jacob along with his caravan (Genesis 31:25). However, Laban had been warned by God in a dream to speak neither good nor bad to Jacob (Genesis 31:24). Following a somewhat contentious meeting between Laban and Jacob, they made a covenant and set a heap of stones as a marker beyond which neither would pass in pursuit of each other. The next morning, Laban departed (Genesis 31:26-54).

Jacob and his caravan set out for Canaan. On the way, he met the angels of God and he decreed "this is God's camp" (Genesis 32:1-2). It is from this point that Jacob developed a plan to communicate and reconcile with his brother Esau. Jacob sent messengers to greet Esau in the land of Seir in Edom. When the messengers returned, they informed Jacob that Esau and 400 men were coming to meet him.

Jacob became fearful. Out of this fear he began plotting and praying. Jacob spent a restless night wrestling with God. Jacob sent his household and goods ahead, and he alone remained to wrestle with a man until daybreak (Genesis 32:22-24.) Interestingly, the New King James version of this passage capitalizes the word Man. In their wrestling, the Man touched Jacob's hip and set it out of joint. But Jacob would not give up until the Man blessed him. It was at this point that God renamed Jacob[1] and gave him the new name Israel.[2]

> Jacob wrestled with God to cross over into the new. He wrestled through to a new identity as Israel that would ultimately manifest in blessing and destiny as Israel, his household, his family, 12 tribes, and ultimately a nation.

God spoke to Jacob again in Genesis 35:9-13 to confirm Jacob's new name as Israel. In this meeting, God also blessed

---

[1] *All the names in the Bible*. (2014). Nashville, TN: Thomas Nelson, 326.
[2] Ibid, 315.

and commissioned Israel in the same manner that He had previously commissioned Adam and Eve, Noah and Abraham. Israel was commissioned to fruitfulness and increase to the extent that nations and kings would come from him. God also promised the land that He gave to Abraham would be his and belong to his descendants.

The commissioning of Israel is simply another affirmation that God has a foundational strategic purpose for households, bets.

Generational Transition

The remaining chapters in the Book of Genesis are prophetic regarding God's intent for His covenant household. With the reconciliation of Israel and Esau in Genesis, chapter 32, a new season is ushered in. Jacob/Israel's life story is told in the remaining chapters of Genesis, a story of both generational and geographical transition.

Israel's transition is demonstrated vividly in a series of dramatic events. In the process of giving birth to Benjamin, Jacobs's 12th son, Jacob's wife, Rachel died. Later, Israel's father Isaac died and was buried by his two sons, Esau and Isaac, as recorded in Genesis, chapter 35.

As Genesis, chapter 37, unfolds, Joseph, the 11th Son of Jacob, becomes the next generation focal point of Scripture. An older generation has passed from the scene and a new generation now takes the stage.

No longer in Paddan Aram, Israel's journey with his mishpaha led him back to Canaan, the land of Abraham. But Israel's journey would take a lengthy detour into Egypt before the descendants of Israel could ultimately call Canaan their possession. According to God's word to Abraham, his descendants would live in exile for 400 years (Genesis 15:13). Israel and his sons lived out the end of their days in Egypt.

Joseph – The Seer and Administrator

The development and accomplishments of Joseph as a next generation seer and administrator are essential to the preservation of Jacob's mishpaha and the prophetic destiny of Israel. The details of Joseph's tumultuous journey from the pit of betrayal to the palace and royal power are found in Genesis, chapters 37; 39-41.

Joseph experienced many adversities, to say the least. Joseph's personal immaturity as a young man and his brothers' jealousy did not make life any easier for him (Genesis 37:1-11). When Joseph shared prophetic dreams that portrayed him as ruling over his brothers, things went from bad to worse. His brothers came to hate Joseph to the point of selling him into slavery (Genesis 37:26-28).

Joseph was ultimately taken to Egypt and sold to Potiphar, the captain of the palace guard (Genesis 39:1). Potiphar's wife became attracted to Joseph and attempted to seduce him. When Joseph ran from her, she accused him of attempted sexual assault (Genesis 39:7-18). Despite the fact that Potiphar's house had prospered under Joseph's control (Genesis 39:5-6), Potiphar was enraged by his wife's accusation and had Joseph thrown into prison (Genesis 39:19-20).

However, the Lord's favor continued to rest upon Joseph, even in prison. The anointing of favor was so powerfully manifested upon Joseph that the prison warden selected Joseph to be in charge of the prisoners and the prison's operations. Joseph was successful in all that he did (Genesis 39: 21-23).

The king's chief baker and chief cupbearer were also in prison with Joseph. They each had a dream on the same night. Upon hearing the dreams, Joseph interpreted them both (Genesis 40:1-23). The cupbearer's dream prophesied his return to Pharaoh's service. The baker's dream prophesied that he would be hanged. Joseph asked the cupbearer to remember him and help obtain his release when the cupbearer was restored to serve in Pharaoh's house.

As Joseph said, the cupbearer was restored to Pharaoh's house and the baker was hanged, but Joseph remained in prison. The cupbearer didn't remember about

Joseph for two years (Genesis 41:1-13). Upon learning that Pharaoh had dreamed two troubling dreams; dreams that none of his advisers could interpret, the cupbearer finally remembered Joseph. Upon the cupbearer's recommendation, Pharaoh sent for Joseph and rehearsed his dreams to Joseph. Hearing Pharaoh's dreams, Joseph provided the interpretation. Joseph interpreted the dreams to speak prophetically about a time to come when seven years of abundance would be upon the land; to be followed by seven years of famine.

The Lord gave Joseph a strategy to conserve the harvest from the years of plenty to provide food during the years of famine. When Pharaoh heard of this strategy, he decided to implement it and appointed Joseph to direct its operation throughout Egypt. Joseph literally went overnight from being a prisoner to becoming second in command in the land of Egypt (Genesis 41:28-43).

The events occurred as Joseph had prophesied. Egypt, under Joseph's leadership had stored the abundance from the seven years of plenty to prepare for seven years of famine. All countries of the world came to buy grain from Joseph as the famine was severe. The famine was so far reaching as to affect the house of Jacob in Canaan (Genesis 41:56-57, 42:1-2).

Learning there was grain in Egypt, Jacob sent his sons to purchase grain for their mishpaha. It was in this transaction the process of reconciliation between Joseph and his brothers was initiated. As a benefit of this reconciliation, Pharaoh extended the hospitality of Egypt to the house of Jacob. Pharaoh offered Jacob's household the best of Egypt, including the best of the land (Genesis 45:16-20).

In the genealogy of Israel's descendants who went to Egypt, we find that Israel had grown from being a household, bet, into being a family, mishpaha. The listing of grandsons in the house of Judah serve as evidence that the sons of Israel had increased and produced a new generation (Genesis 46:8-27).

Israel lived in Egypt 17 years and died when he was 147 years old (Genesis 47:28). By the time of the death of

Israel, Jacob's mishpaha had produced what would become known as the 12 tribes, matteh, of Israel (Genesis 49: 28).

Joseph lived to be 110 years. He lived to see the third generation of Ephraim, his son's children. Before his death, Joseph prophesied that Israel would leave Egypt and return to the land promised to Abraham (Genesis 50:24). At Joseph's request, upon his death he was embalmed and placed in a coffin. His bones were to be carried to Canaan on Israel's departure from Egypt.

Household Grace

God's covenant is a covenant of grace. Family iniquity and dysfunction are not too much for the One who has chosen to be known as "the God of Abraham, Isaac and Jacob" (Exodus 3:6).

> He has shown you, O man, what is good;
> And what does the Lord require of you
> But to do justly,
> To love mercy, And to walk humbly with your
> God?
>
> Micah 6:8

The Households of Genesis: Conclusion

The households we have examined thus far have numerous commonalities. None were perfect in all their ways all the time. They had obvious faults and failures. But they had encounters, conversations and relationship with God. God spoke, and they responded. They birthed what they were called to birth in spite of bareness and delay. They multiplied and prospered as each was commissioned to do so. They became the foundation that God would use to bring reconciliation, deliverance and salvation into the world. They became the vehicle God would use to manifest His "Only Begotten Son" (John 3:16), the "Last Adam" (1 Corinthians 15:45).

CHAPTER 4

A Nation and Its Destiny

Moses and the Exodus

Following the death of Joseph, the descendants of Jacob remained in Egypt for many generations. Exodus 12:40 tells us that Israel lived in Egypt for a total of 430 years. From the original 70 members of Jacob's family, Israel multiplied greatly in Egypt. The enormity of Israel's growth came to provoke fear in the heart of Pharaoh, the ruler of Egypt.

The Egyptians began to oppress the Israelites and "set taskmasters over them to afflict them" (Exodus 1:11). But, Israel continued to multiply and grow in spite of the affliction they experienced at the hands of the Egyptians. In an effort to stop Israel's population growth, the king of Egypt asked the midwives to kill all of the newborn males of Israel (Exodus 1:15-16). But, the midwives feared God and did not carry out the command to kill the boy babies of Israel. The growth of Israel became such a problem to the Egyptians that Pharaoh commanded the people to cast every newborn Hebrew son into the river (Exodus 1:22).

Exodus 2:1-10 records the story of the birth and early life of Moses, the next significant figure in the history of the household of Jacob and the nation of Israel. As a baby, Moses was hidden in the bulrushes in a specially prepared waterproof basket to protect him from the murderous intent of the Egyptians. If you have read this story, you understand that only God could orchestrate the events that led to Moses' early nurture and education. Moses' mother was hired by Pharaoh's daughter to nurse and care for him. Moses became the adopted son of Pharaoh's daughter to be raised as royalty.

But, Moses had a destiny and a calling. His future was not to live in the palace of Pharaoh and simply ignore the fact that Israel was being oppressed. One day as a grown man, Moses saw an Egyptian beating a Hebrew; Moses killed the Egyptian. When Moses discovered that his crime had been found out, he fled to the land of Midian where he married the daughter of the Midian priest and served as a shepherd to the flocks of his father-in-law (Exodus 3:1).

As time passed, the Israelites cried out to the God of Abraham, Isaac and Jacob in their oppression by the Egyptians, and God heard them. In answer to the prayers of the Israelites, God sent Moses and his brother Aaron to Pharaoh, ruler of Egypt, to request Israel's release to travel into the wilderness to worship (Exodus 7:16). Moses was 80-years old and Aaron was 83 when they approached Pharaoh with this request (Exodus 7:7).

Exodus, chapters 5–12, records the story of Moses and Aaron's confrontations with Pharaoh on behalf of Israel. Scripture records signs and wonders and plagues that God brought against Egypt in the effort to free His people from their oppressors. However, Pharaoh's heart grew harder with each of Moses and Aaron's requests for Israel's freedom. The execution of nine terrible plagues did not soften Pharaoh's resolve.

However, God assured Moses a tenth plague would be the final plague. Following the tenth plague, Israel would indeed be released from Pharaoh's grip (Exodus 11:1). Again, the Lord prepared Israel for the execution of another plague of judgment against Egypt, the tenth and concluding plague, the death of every firstborn in Egypt (Exodus 11:1-5).

The tenth plague is associated with the commemoration of the Passover as instituted in Exodus, chapters 12 and 13. Each Hebrew household was given specific instructions regarding the preparation required for the Passover. Included in these instructions, each household was required to sacrifice an unblemished lamb (Exodus 12:3-5). The blood of this lamb was to be spread upon the doorposts of their homes. On the evening of the final plague, Israel was instructed to gather by household and eat the meat (or body) of the lamb. In their obedience to prepare according to all of the instructions of the Lord, the households of Israel would be "passed over" by the death that came upon the households of the Egyptians. Although the Passover brought judgment upon Egypt, it brought redemption, release and deliverance to Israel.

Following the tenth plague, the Egyptians were eager to be rid of the Hebrews. The Egyptians gave the Israelites whatever they asked for in order to send them speedily on their way (Exodus 12:30-36).

Moving Forward in Household Alignment

Passover was the beginning, not the end; simply the starting line for Israel's journey to the Promised Land. During this journey, a mass of former slaves became a nation of worshippers and warriors, but not overnight. What could have been an 11-day journey became a 40-year delay (Deuteronomy 1:2-3). Ultimately, the blessing that one generation failed to receive because of unbelief became the possession of the following generation (Deuteronomy 1:35-39; Joshua 1:6).

Yet, in all of its wanderings and rebellion, Israel did not cast aside its family foundation. Israel's hierarchal family structure retained its relevance and significance throughout Israel's journey into its destiny.

During their journey, with instructions from the Lord, Israel encamped around the Tabernacle in the wilderness in a set order by household, family and tribe (Numbers 2:34). According to Strong's Concordance, the Hebrew family words bet, mishpaha and matteh are used to describe the encampment's arrangement of Israel in Numbers, chapter 2.

The family structure becomes apparent again as Moses assigned the boundaries of Canaan and various allotments of land to each Israelite tribe in Numbers, chapter 34.

In moving beyond the wilderness and into its Promised Land, Israel maintained its foundational family alignment, the relational alignment of household, family, tribe and nation.

Jericho and the Genealogy of Jesus

Jericho forms a very interesting intersection in Israel's household history. Following a 40-year season of delay, Israel finally entered into the Promised Land (Joshua, chapter 1). As Israel began the process of possessing its destiny, it produced a very interesting entry into the bloodline of Abraham, David and ultimately into the genealogy of Jesus. Matthew 1:5-6, records this entry, "Salmon begot Boaz by Rahab, Boaz begot Obed by Ruth, Obed begot Jesse, and Jesse begot David the king." This Scripture is worthy of notice because it places two women in the genealogy of Jesus. And, secondly, one of those women had apparently been known as a prostitute.

Prior to Israel's entry into the Promised Land, Joshua, Moses' successor as leader of Israel, sent two spies into the land. They were instructed to "view the land, especially Jericho." At Jericho the spies met a woman identified in Scripture as "a harlot named Rahab" (Joshua 2:1). If you carefully read Matthew's genealogy above, you might have noticed that Rahab became David's great-great-grandmother. Only with God is this possible, as it broke all the traditional rules!

Scripture notes that Rahab hid the Israelite spies and did not betray them. In return for this kindness, the spies promised to spare Rahab's family when the Lord delivered Jericho into the hands of Israel (Joshua 2:12-14).

When Jericho fell and the two spies went to honor their promise to Rahab, their instructions from Joshua (Joshua 6:22) were to "go into the harlot's house," her bet.[1] But, when

---

[1] Strong, James. *Strongs Exhaustive Concordance* Grand Rapids, MI: Baker Book House, 1983. H1004.

they carried out the instructions to "bring out all that she has," they brought out Rahab, her father, mother, brothers and "all who belonged to her," her mishpaha[1] or family (Joshua 6:23).

> How does a woman, a harlot become David's great, great grandmother and become forever listed in the genealogy of Jesus?

Scripture records that Rahab made a confession of faith, "the Lord your God, He is God in heaven above and on earth beneath" (Joshua 2:11).

In the New Testament, the writer of Hebrews clearly states, "By faith the harlot Rahab did not perish with those who did not believe, when she had received the spies with peace" (Hebrews 11:31). Rahab entered Jesus' bloodline by faith.

But Rahab's faith and corresponding actions did not bring deliverance simply for Rahab alone as an individual. She brought blessing to her household and family. A woman, a harlot, named Rahab found blessing, redemption and honor as she entered into the bloodline of David and Jesus by faith in the Lord God of Heaven and Earth.

The Boaz Blessing

Boaz was born into the tribe of Judah and the household of Salmon (his father) to Rahab (his mother), a Canaanite (Matthew 1:2-5). Although the Old Testament is patriarchal and Jewish by nature, the story of Boaz is strongly intertwined with the narrative of three women, Rahab, Naomi and Ruth; only one was Jewish. You may note Rahab and Ruth, the non-Jews, are included in Matthew's genealogy of Jesus.

The story of Boaz is told in the Book of Ruth. As the narrative of the Book of Ruth unfolds, Naomi, her husband and her two sons have relocated from Bethlehem in Judah to

---

[1] Ibid, H4940.

Moab due to a famine in the land (Ruth 1:1). While in Moab, Naomi's husband, Elimelech, died. However, as a widow, Naomi still had her two sons.

The two sons, Mahlon and Kilion, took Moabite wives. Naomi's daughters-in-law were Orpah and Ruth (Ruth 1:4). However, after about ten years, both of Naomi's sons died. Naomi found herself in a foreign land, a widow with two Moabite daughters-in-law.

Naomi then received news that the Lord had come to the aid of her people and food was available in her homeland of Judah. At this, Naomi, Orpah and Ruth set out on the journey to Judah, but Naomi convinced Orpah to turn back (Ruth 1:6-14). Ruth, pledged her lifelong loyalty to Naomi. In Ruth's pledge of loyalty to Naomi, she also pledged allegiance to Naomi's people and to Naomi's God (Ruth 1:16-17).

Scripture does not tell us where Ruth and Naomi lived upon their return to Bethlehem. What we do know is that Naomi and Ruth needed a source of provision. Ruth's answer to the situation was to join the barley harvest and glean the fields after the reapers. As Ruth began gleaning, she found herself gleaning in the field of Boaz, a relative of Naomi's deceased husband, Elimelech (Ruth 2:1-3). Boaz is described as "a man of great wealth." Boaz noticed Ruth gleaning in his fields and treated her with favor and kindness (Ruth 2:5-16).

Scripture takes note of the noble character and loyalty of Ruth (Ruth 2:11-12; 3:10-11). However, at this point it is the character, kindness and wisdom of Boaz that activates God's household redemption strategy and intersects the genealogy of Jesus. Boaz agreed to assume the role of Ruth's "Kinsman Redeemer" (Ruth 3:12-13; 4:9-10).

As applied in the case of Naomi, Ruth and Boaz, the principal of the "Kinsman Redeemer" requires a close male relative to produce an heir by the widow of the deceased kinsman who is without offspring (Deuteronomy 25:5-10). In this case, Boaz agreed to purchase the estate of Elimelech, Kilion and Mahlon. This purchase, or redemption, also required that he take Ruth as his wife in order to maintain the name of Mahlon.

In his agreement to become the Kinsman Redeemer in this story, Boaz models the role of Jesus as our Kinsman Redeemer. We have been redeemed by the Blood of Jesus (Ephesians 1:7). In Christ, there is restoration of household, inheritance and destiny.

David —The Household of a King

David is first introduced by name in the Book of Ruth (4:17, 22). However, we are introduced to his household and his selection as king in 1 Samuel, chapter 16. Following the failure of Saul (1 Samuel, chapter 15), God sent the Prophet Samuel on a mission to anoint a new king over Israel. Samuel was instructed that the new king would be among the sons of the household of Jesse of Bethlehem (1 Samuel 16:1).

Imagine, if you will, that you are Jesse. Imagine waking up one morning in Bethlehem in your household of eight boys without any inkling that the prophet is on his way to your house, and certainly no thought as to why he might be coming. Just the very appearance of the prophet in Bethlehem sent shudders through the hearts of the elders of the town (1 Samuel 16:4).

Think of the prophet coming to the door and putting you and your sons through the process necessary to be considered ceremonially clean[1] (1 Samuel 16:5 KJV). The prophet considered each of Jesse's seven eldest sons, but Samuel did not see the Lord's anointed among these seven (1 Samuel 16:10). When the prophet asked, Jesse revealed that there was yet another son, the youngest son, who was tending sheep.

The prophet allowed no one to sit until the youngest son was brought before him. When David, Jesse's youngest son, appeared, the Lord spoke to Samuel, "Arise, anoint him;

---

[1] Strong, James. *Strongs Exhaustive Concordance* Grand Rapids, MI: Baker Book House, 1983, H6942.

for this is the one!" (1 Samuel 16:12). When Samuel anointed David with oil, the Holy Spirit came upon David powerfully (1 Samuel 16:13).

Saul did not surrender the crown or throne just because Samuel anointed David to be king. The task of assuming the throne over Judah and Israel required a process that transpired over a period of years. Between the time of his anointing by Samuel and assuming the throne of all Judah and Israel, many significant events occurred in David's life. Over this period, David would cease to be known as a shepherd boy and become known as a military hero. The women of Israel danced and sang, "Saul has slain his thousands, and David his tens of thousands" (1 Samuel 18:7, NIV). Hearing this enraged Saul and provoked his jealousy towards David (1 Samuel 18:8-9).

As recorded in 1 Samuel, chapters 18-26, Saul initiated a series of attempts to kill David. Scripture does not indicate precisely how long Saul pursued David. However, because of Saul's murderous intent, David entered a season of life as a fugitive. Although he had been anointed as king, David became a man on the run.

Ziklag – On the Path to the Throne

Ultimately, David determined that he would be safer in the land of the Philistines, Israel's historic enemies, than in Israel (1 Samuel 27:1). The time period that had elapsed between David's anointing and his entry into the land of the Philistines is not definitively known. Suffice it to say, David had been on the run long enough to allow him to acquire both a family and a military troop. When he fled into the land of the Philistines, David had two wives, 600 men and each had his household, bet, with him (1 Samuel 27:2-3). In that time of history, the Philistines lived in a coastal strip between the Mediterranean and the land of Israel and Judah known as Philistia.[1]

---

[1] https://www.britannica.com/topic/Philistine-people/media/1/456536/3078. Accessed 9/15/2019.

Scripture does not indicate that David sought the Lord's advice about his exile in the land of the Philistines. It would appear that this plan was born out of fear and the conclusions of David's own mind (1 Samuel 27:1).

In Israel's history, it is not unusual for God's chosen ones to go into a foreign land for a season for their provision and protection. Abraham went to Egypt; Isaac went to Gerar; Jacob went to Paddan Aram; Joseph and the household of Israel dwelled in Egypt; Moses went to the backside of the desert; Naomi and her household went to Moab. Matthew 2:13 informs us that Joseph was instructed by the angel of the Lord to take Mary and Jesus to Egypt for a season to escape the treachery of Herod. As with his ancestors, the land of his exile was not David's inheritance or destiny.

Scripture records that David's strategy worked. When Saul learned that David had fled to Gath in the land of the Philistines, Saul no longer pursued David (1 Samuel 27:4).

In the land of the Philistines, David found favor with Achish, King of Gath. David presented a request to Achish for a place to dwell, a place in a country town away from the royal city and Achish's eye. Achish responded to David's request favorably by granting the town of Ziklag (1 Samuel 27:5-6).

David and his band of fighting men were warriors. Ziklag served as a base of operation for David and his troop to launch raids on the Geshurites, the Girzites and the Amalekites, peoples who lived in the land extending to Shur and Egypt. As a guest in Philistine territory, David had to act with subtlety and shrewdness in his raiding incursions. Achish, David's host, questioned David regarding his raiding activities. The language of 1 Samuel 27:10-12, tends to indicate that David did not fully disclose the exact nature and location of these raids to Achish. It appears that David explained his activities in a diplomatic manner so as not to displease Achish. From David's explanation, Achish came to the conclusion that, by the nature of his raids, David was making himself obnoxious to Israel. In this, Achish concluded that David intended to always be his servant.

The Agony of Household Loss and Grace to Recover All

Achish and the Philistines gathered to fight against Israel. Achish requested that David join him in this fight and David agreed (1 Samuel 28:1-2). However, the Philistine military commanders would not allow a former Israeli military hero to go into this battle (1 Samuel 29:3-5). In response to the Philistine commander's request, Achish sent David and his men away (1 Samuel 29:10).

On the third day of their march back to Ziklag, David and his men returned home to find that the Amalekites had burned and looted the town. David and his men also discovered that the Amalekites had taken their wives, sons and daughters captive and went on their way (1 Samuel 30:1-3).

Prior to this time, David and his men were pursuing "their thing." One of the things I learned many years ago is that a strength that is overplayed becomes a weakness. These men were warriors going out to war; that's what kings and their warriors did in that day (2 Samuel 11:1). David and his men were so focused on the fight before them that they neglected to set a rear guard to protect the people and possessions that were most valuable and dearest in their lives.

Ziklag is a reminder that whatever our vocation, calling or gifting may be, it should not overshadow our responsibility to serve and protect our household. The failure to protect our household provides the adversary an open door to attack and plunder. This is a "backdoor" strategy of the evil one to defeat the effectiveness of our anointing. It is a strategy that almost worked. David's people were so grieved at their loss that they considered stoning him (1 Samuel 30:6).

But, David is an example of an overcomer. When he had lost everything and his people thought of stoning him, Scripture records that David encouraged himself in the Lord and sought the Lord's will (1 Samuel 30:6-8). The word of the

Lord for David was, "Pursue, for you shall surely overtake them and without fail recover all" (1 Samuel 30:8).

To David and his men, pursue meant to get out of Ziklag! Don't stay in the place of grief, doubt and despair. Recovery from a great loss usually requires courage and intentionality to move beyond.

Recovery requires endurance. David left 200 men at the Brook of Besor because they were too exhausted to continue (1 Samuel 30:9-10). But, even with 200 fewer men in his troop, David continued the pursuit of recovery.

As they continued their pursuit, David and his band of 400, discovered an Egyptian servant who had become ill and left behind by the Amalekites. The young man was able to lead David directly to the ones who had looted Ziklag (1 Samuel 30:11-16). The revelation David needed in the journey to recovery was provided as he faithfully pursued the process of recovery.

However, the Amalekites did not give up their plunder without a battle. At the end of the journey, recovery required a fight to finish. David and his troop battled from dusk of one day until the evening of the next. As the Lord had promised, David recovered all (1 Samuel 30:17-19).

With this victory and the spoils secured, David and his men returned to Ziklag (1 Samuel 30:26). With the recovery of the spoils of the Amalekites, David's wait to become king was nearing an end.

Saul was severely wounded in battle with the Philistines and fell on his own sword rather than be taken captive (1 Samuel 31:4-5). With the death of Saul, the next chapter of David's life began to unfold and Ziklag became simply another stop on the way to the throne of Israel.

Scriptures states that David inquired of the Lord, and the Lord instructed him to relocate to Hebron in Judah. David, his wives, his fighting men and their households moved to Hebron and the surrounding area.

At Hebron the elders of Judah anointed David

as King of Judah (2 Samuel 2:4). David reigned over Judah for seven and one-half years in Hebron before the elders of Israel came to Hebron to anoint him as their king (2 Samuel 5:1-4).

David was 30-years old when he started to reign. As a side note and an interesting comparison, Jesus was 30-years old when He launched His ministry (Luke 3:23).

David's Family Focus

Before leaving this section, it is important to note David was anointed by the prophet within the context of Jesse's household. He was anointed by the men of Judah as ruler over the household, or bet, of Judah (2 Samuel 2:4). In the context of extended family, elders from all of Israel's tribes also came to Hebron to anoint David as Israel's ruler (2 Samuel 5:1-3).

Once again in David's ascent to the throne of Israel, we see:

1. Relational leadership is the centerpiece of God's strategy for prosperity, multiplication and stewardship of households, families, tribes and nations.
2. The manifestation of our Kingdom identity is a birthing process that requires us to go through:
   a. Conception: Samuel's anointing.
   b. Gestation: The years between Samuel's anointing and the anointing of Judah.
   c. Emerging: Crowning began with the anointing of David as the King of Judah and the birthing phase was completed with his anointing as King of Israel.

David's Household Blessing

In 2 Samuel, chapter 7, the Lord's blessing of David is delivered by the Prophet Nathan (2 Samuel 7:4-16). There are noticeable instances of similarity between the blessing of

David and the blessing of Abraham found in Genesis 12:1-3; 17:6-9.

1. God promised both Abraham and David that He would make their name great.
2. God promised both Abraham and David that He would give them land, a place to dwell.
3. God promised both Abraham and David that He would give them offspring and their descendants would sit on the throne to rule as king.
4. Both Abraham and David's descendants were required to keep covenant with Him.

The early years of David's reign over Israel were glorious and great. David captured Jerusalem and established it as the seat of government (2 Samuel 5:6-12). He was victorious in battle over the Philistines at Baal Perazim (2 Samuel 5:17-25) and achieved other notable military victories as well (2 Samuel 8:1-14; 10:1-19). David brought the Ark of the Covenant into Jerusalem, and worship was established there (2 Samuel 6:1-19). David honored his covenant with Jonathan, son of Saul (1 Samuel 18:3-4) in his care and blessing of Mephibosheth, Jonathan's disabled son (2 Samuel 9:1-13).

However; as with Adam and Eve in the Garden, a dark day came when David followed his flesh and spiritually opened the door to iniquity in his household.

David and Bathsheba – Bloodline Redemption

The events of David's adulterous affair with Bathsheba and his murderous plot to bring about the death of Bathsheba's husband, Uriah the Hittite, are recorded in 2 Samuel, chapter 11. These events seem uncharacteristic and out of place with David's history. They defy the reality that David, Bathsheba and their son, Solomon, are noted in Matthew's genealogy of Jesus, the Messiah, the Son of God (Matthew 1:6). Luke's Gospel seems to further this paradox by noting that Jesus would sit on the throne of His father David (Luke 1:31-32).

Even the Apostle Paul clearly references the Savior as the descendant of David (Acts 13:20-23).

> How can this be? How can an adulterer, murderer and adulteress escape punishment under Levitical Law? How can one whose crimes are as heinous as these become included in the house and lineage of Jesus? The punishment set out in the letter of the Law would appear to require that both David and Bathsheba be put to death.
>
> Leviticus 20:10

In searching the Scriptures for an answer, it seems that the same context applies here as in the case of the woman taken in adultery in John 8:3-11. In this, I believe that Holy Spirit reveals an interesting point of law that is applied in both instances. Under the Law, a person could not be convicted of any crime or offense by the testimony of only one witness. The testimony of two or three witnesses was required for a conviction (Deuteronomy 19:15). In both instances, David and Bathsheba as well as the woman taken in adultery, guilt was present; however, there were not enough witnesses willing to testify against them to result in their death sentence.

In the case of the unidentified woman taken in adultery, "When Jesus had raised Himself up and saw no one but the woman, He said to her, "'Woman, where are those accusers of yours? Has no one condemned you?' She said, 'No one, Lord.' And Jesus said to her, Neither do I condemn you; go and sin no more"" (John 8:10-11).

Jesus's words and actions reflect the Father's heart (John 5:19). His verdict in the adulterous woman's case mirrors God's heart in the case of David and Bathsheba.

It is important to note that from his confrontation by the Prophet Nathan (2 Samuel 12:1-14), David's repentance is expressed in Psalm 51. David admitted his sin, repented and earnestly sought God's forgiveness. David did not make excuses.

> David said to Nathan, "I have sinned against the Lord." And Nathan said to David, "The Lord also has put away your sin; you shall not die."
>
> 2 Samuel 12:13

In the midst of judgment, David found mercy. Although he was not stoned to death for his transgression of the Law, David did not escape the consequences of his sin. As with Adam and Eve and their sin in Genesis, chapter 3, David's sin did not solely impact David alone; it had consequences for his household and bloodline. The prophet Nathan announced, "The sword shall never depart your house." David's own household would turn against him; bring calamity upon him, and one in his own household would openly have sex with his wives in broad daylight (2 Samuel 12:10-12; 16:21-5822).

As a further punishment, the child conceived by David and Bathsheba's adulterous affair was struck by an illness and died (2 Samuel 12:15-18). David's sin had opened a door to the spirit of adultery and murder that had only started to activate death and destruction in his household.

David's son, Amnon, raped his sister Tamar (2 Samuel 13:1-16). David's son, Absalom, killed Amnon, in revenge of the rape of Tamar (2 Samuel 13: 23-33). Later, Absalom attempted to overthrow David as king (2 Samuel 15:1-12). Absalom successfully forced David to flee Jerusalem (2 Samuel 15:13-22); took over David's palace and had sex with David's concubines on the palace roof in sight of the all Israel (2 Samuel 16:21-22). Ultimately, Absalom died by accidental hanging when his hair became entangled in branches of a tree (2 Samuel 18:9-10).

Solomon – Treachery and Transition

Again, intrigue enters the narrative. As David grew old, his son, Adonijah, conspired to become the next king of Israel (1

Kings 1:5). However, David and Bathsheba had a son named Solomon. Scripture records, "The Lord loved him" (2 Samuel 12:24). Ultimately, Solomon became king of Israel, but not without plotting and collaboration between Bathsheba and the Prophet Nathan. Together, Bathsheba and Nathan secured the appointment of Solomon as king (1 Kings 1:9-39). Solomon became the son of David that is included in the genealogy of Jesus (Matthew 1:6).

Lesson Learned

In this narrative, we again see the impact of parental sin upon a household and a nation. We see the manifestation of the sins of David, the father, transmitted in the generations of his bloodline. This becomes even more apparent in the later life of Solomon and his offspring.

We also see the impact of repentance. The story of David is another testimony of household recovery and restoration by the God of mercy and grace. In Jesus, the Son of David (Matthew 1:1), we see the ultimate redemption and restoration of David's identity, inheritance and destiny. It is in Christ that all who have sinned and missed the mark find household, bloodline restoration.

> Mercy and truth have met together;
> righteousness and peace have kissed.
>
> Psalm 85:10

CHAPTER 5

From Old to New

Continuing the Household Foundation

In the account of Messiah as told in the Gospel record of Matthew, Mark, Luke and John, Israel was encapsulated by a Roman occupation that manifested itself in a variety of forms, including military might and a dictatorial political structure. Roman military and political leaders tolerated Hebrew worship, but only to the extent that it helped maintain the peace of the region and did not interfere with the exercise of Roman authority.

The authority and power of Rome is vividly exhibited in the events surrounding the birth of Jesus as recorded in Luke 2:1-3. Joseph and Mary, in the final months of her pregnancy, were required to travel from Nazareth in Galilee to Bethlehem of Judea because of a census decreed by Caesar Augustus, the first emperor of the Roman Empire.

As we have established earlier in this writing, in the Old Testament, God's covenant people, Israel, functioned as a society rooted in a hierarchal family structure: household, family, tribe, and nation; bet, mishpaha, mattah or matteh, and goy. The story of Mary and Joseph also illustrates this pattern and its continued practice in Hebrew family life into the time of Jesus. Joseph and Mary were required to travel to Bethlehem, "because he (Joseph) was of the house and lineage of David" (Luke 2:4). The household of Mary and Joseph were connected by family bloodline into the household of David and the tribe of Judah (Matthew 1:3-17). This was a reality that not even Rome would ignore.

The entire New Testament account is a testimony to the place, power and authority of household to carry and multiply the life and gospel of Messiah in the midst of a world order that is controlled by politics, military might and corrupt religious structures.

Mary, Joseph and Jesus

Even though Jesus was born in a Bethlehem manger, He was born into a bet. The power of the Highest overshadowed Mary (Luke 1:35) and she conceived, but it was important to God that His only begotten Son would be birthed into a bet. An angel of the Lord appeared to Joseph in a dream and authorized him to take Mary as his wife. When Joseph woke up, he did exactly what the angel of the Lord had commanded him and took Mary home as his wife (Matthew 1: 24 AMP).

In the Matthew the New Testament, home or house is translated from the Greek word oikos. Oikos can be translated as household or family.[1] Functionally, Mary and Joseph became a Jewish bet and a Greek oikos.

Whether Old Testament or New Testament; whether bet or oikos; whether Adam and Eve or Mary and Joseph, household or family is the foundation God has formed for life, faith and purpose for all of humankind under both the Old and New Covenant.

Aligned for Worship

In this coming season, how we align for worship is a key to unlocking God's plan for redemption, deliverance and destiny

---

[1] Vine, William Edwyn, Merrill Frederick Unger, and William White. Vines Expository Dictionary of Biblical Words. Nashville: T. Nelson, 1985. p313

on multiple levels. As we shall see in this section, the place or locations of worship as outlined in the New Testament also flow in harmony with God's alignment of Israel around the Tabernacle in the wilderness. As Israel camped around the Tabernacle, they did so as a nation in alignment by tribe, family and household (Numbers 2:1-34).

> In the New Testament, we find a very distinct pattern for the places of ministry and worship as practiced by Jesus, His disciples and the Early Church. It is not by coincidence, that this pattern aligns with the Bet, Mishpaha, Matteh, Goy alignment of the Hebrew Old Testament.

Jesus, His disciples and the Early Church worshipped and ministered:

1. In homes, or worship and ministry in Bet.
2. In synagogues, or worship in families or multiple Bets.
3. In the temple, a place of tribal and national worship and ministry.
4. To gatherings of the masses in locations beyond the bounds of religious tradition.

The Home Ministry of Jesus

The ministry of Jesus presents overwhelming evidence that ministry should have a household focus.

1. Jesus' first miracle was performed in a family/household setting at a wedding He had attended with His mother in Cana of Galilee (John 2:1-11).
2. Jesus healed Peter's mother-in-law, delivered many who were demon possessed and healed many at Peter's house (Matthew 8:14-17).
3. Jesus ate with publicans and sinners at Matthew's house (Matthew 9:9-13).

4. Jairus' daughter was healed in a house (Matthew 9:23-26; Mark 5:35-43; Luke 8:49-56).

5. When Jesus sent out the 12 to preach, He sent them to engage in home-based ministry (Matthew 10:1-13; Luke 9:1-6)

6. When Jesus sent out the 70 to minister two by two, He sent them to engage in home-based ministry (Luke 10:1-12).

7. Jesus taught His disciples privately in a house (Matthew 13:36; Mark 7:17, 9:28).

8. The anointing of Jesus with alabaster perfume occurred in the home of Simon the leper (Matthew 26:6; Mark 14:3; Luke 7:37). Jesus was anointed in a similar fashion by Mary at Lazarus' house (John 12:3).

9. Jesus and His disciples had Passover in a house (Matthew 26:18; Mark 14:14; Luke 22:10-11).

10. Jesus healed the paralytic in a house in Capernaum (Mark 2:1; Luke 5:17-19).

11. The conversion of Zacchaeus occurred in a house (Luke 19:1-10).

12. The Syrophoencian woman came to Jesus to obtain healing for her daughter while Jesus was in a house near Tyre (Mark 7:24-30).

13. Jesus healed the sick in their homes even when He was not physically present in their home (John 4:46-54; Matthew 8:5-13; Luke 7:1-10).

14. After the demoniac of the Gadarenes was delivered, he was instructed to return to his house and tell what God has done (Luke 8:39). Mark's text (Mark 5:19) states this with greater clarity in that Jesus instructed the delivered one to return to his "sou" or "own home."[1]

---

[1] Strong, James. *Strongs Exhaustive Concordance* Grand Rapids, MI: Baker Book House, 1983, G4675.

The Alignment of Holy Spirit, the Church and the House
It is commonly held that the birth of the Church occurred on the Day of Pentecost as recorded in the Book of Acts, chapter 2. The promise of the presence and power of Holy Spirit (Acts 1:8) was fulfilled when the Holy Spirit manifested in the sound of a rushing wind and tongues of fire resting upon approximately 120 believers gathered in a house[1] in Jerusalem (Acts 2:2). Some may refer to this as the Jewish Pentecost.

In Acts, chapter 10, reference is made to the Gentile Pentecost. The Apostle Peter was sent on a special mission to the household of a centurion named Cornelius. Peter did the unthinkable! He entered a gentile house and preached the gospel of Jesus to them. While he was preaching, the Holy Spirit came upon them in a house as a household! (Acts 10:44).

As with the Jewish Pentecost and Gentile Pentecost, *on April 9, 1906, a house, the Los Angeles home of Richard and Ruth Asberry at 216 North Bonnie Brae Street "became known as the spot where the modern Pentecostal movement began."[2]*

The of Household and the First Century Church
As the Church spread beyond Jerusalem, it was "household" that became the foundation of that expansion and the fulfillment of The Great Commission (Matthew 28:16-20; Acts 1:8). The following references testify to this:
1. The conversion of Saul of Tarsus was completed and his blindness was healed in a home in Damascus (Acts 9:1-19).
2. When Peter was miraculously delivered from prison by an angel, he went to the home of Mark's mother where many people were praying (Acts 12:12-17).

[1] Strong, James. Strongs Exhaustive Concordance Grand Rapids, MI: Baker Book House, 1983, G3624.

[2] https://www.challies.com/articles/the-history-of-christianity-in-25-objects-bonnie-brae-house. Accessed 9/15/2019.

3. Through the ministry of Paul in the house of Titius Justus (in Corinth), Crispus, a synagogue ruler, and his household, along with many Corinthians were converted (Acts 18:7-8).

4. Paul preached from house to house in Ephesus (Acts 20:20).

5. In concluding the Book of Romans, Paul greets Priscilla, Acquila and the church that meets in their house (Romans 16:3-5). Paul's final greetings in 1 Corinthians 16:19 also mentions the church that meets in Priscilla and Aquila's house.

6. In his final greetings to the Church at Colossae, he greets Nympha and the church in his house (Colossians 4:15).

7. The conversion of the Philippian Jailer (Acts 16:25-34) is a clear reference to "Household Salvation" and a Biblical focus on home and family.

8. In the Early Church, the home served as the training ground for ministry. As parents raised their children in the nurture and admonition of the Lord, they actually proved their ministry and qualifications as "elders" or leaders of the church. *Paul is clear those who are to have authority in the work of the church should be those who have proven themselves as capable leaders of their "own home"* (1 Timothy 3:4-5, 12).

Jesus in the Synagogue

In Jesus' day, the synagogue was a Jewish place of local worship established around a "minyan" or at least ten adult men.[1] In Nazareth, Jesus' childhood home, He was known in the local synagogue. Luke 4:14-30 records the inauguration of

---

[1] https://www.myjewishlearning.com/article/minyan-the-congregational-quorum. Accessed 9/15/2019.

Jesus' Galilean ministry and His ministry in synagogues.

The Apostles and the Early Church in Synagogues

Over the span of the history of Israel, in the Old Testament, New Testament and modern eras, the Jews have been dispersed into various nations throughout the world. Many Jews fled their homeland during times of oppression and established synagogues as places of worship in places where they settled. By the time of the Early Church, synagogues had been established in various locations across the Roman Empire.

As the early apostles started to minister in these cities, they would seek out a synagogue and minister. Some examples of synagogue ministry by the Early Church fathers would include Antioch in Pisidia (Acts 13:14); Iconium (Acts 14:1); Thessalonica (Acts 17:1); Berea (Acts 17:10), and Ephesus (Acts 18:19).

Jesus and the Temple

Jesus cast the moneychangers out of the temple (Matthew 21:12; Mark 11:15; Luke 19:45; John 2:13-17). Jesus healed in the temple in Jerusalem (Matthew 21:14). Jesus taught in the temple (Matthew 21:23, 26:55; Mark 12:35, 14:49; Luke 19:45, 20:1, 21:37-38, 22:52-53; John 7:28, 8:2, 8:20, 18:20).

Disciples and Early Church Leaders and the Temple

Jesus' disciples worshipped in the temple (Luke 2:13-17); Acts 2:46, 3:1, 5:42). The disciples taught in the temple (Acts 5:20-21). Paul worshipped in the temple (Acts 21:26-30; 22:17).

The Mass Meetings of Jesus and the Early Church

Jesus ministered to the masses in places other than the home, synagogue or temple (Matthew 14:21; 15:38; Mark 6:44, 8:9; Luke 9:14; John 6:10). The Early Church also ministered to the masses (Acts 2:41, 4:4, 5:14-16, 14:1, 15:30, 17:4).

Summary and Conclusion

God's intent for those created in His image has been clearly expressed.

> Be fruitful and multiply; fill the earth and subdue it; have dominion over the fish of the sea, over the birds of the air, and over every living thing that moves on the earth.
>
> Genesis 1:28

As a household, Adam and Eve were commissioned to become parents, and become profitable stewards of all of God's creation. The foundational stewardship of God's dominion was vested in the household of Adam and Eve.

The pattern of worship, discipleship and ministry as demonstrated in the life of Jesus and the Early Church continued in alignment with this original intent. The household was the foundation of phenomenal fruitfulness and multiplication of the gospel in the Early Church era.

Important Note

It is not the purpose of this section to discourage believers from worshipping Jesus in congregational or mass worship settings. The purpose of this section is to encourage the body of Christ in the modern era to rediscover and reconnect with its relational household root, with its foundation for life, fruitfulness, multiplication and authority wherever, whenever and however it may gather in His name.

CHAPTER 6

The Power of Choice!

If it seems evil to you to serve the
Lord, choose for yourselves this day
whom you will serve, whether the
gods which your fathers served that
were on the other side of the River, or
the gods of the Amorites, in whose
land you dwell.
But as for me and my house, we will
serve the Lord.

Joshua 24:15

The value of personal choice, as for me
The words of the last two chapters of the Book of
Joshua are the last words of Joshua before his death.
As he stood before Israel that day, he did not simply
speak with the authority of his position or title. His
words were anchored in a life of unshakable faith and
personal integrity. Joshua spoke that day as a man
whose words carried great power with God. It is likely
that many in this audience could recall a day when
Joshua spoke to the sun and moon, and time stood still

(Joshua 10:12-14).

When Joshua spoke that day, his words of instruction and warning were not merely the rhetorical comment of a statesman. They were an authentic testimony to his personal determination and dedication to serve the Lord regardless of the decision of others, a determination and dedication that Joshua had demonstrated on more than one occasion.

When the Israelites rebelled against the Lord and worshipped the golden calf at Mount Sinai (Exodus 32:1-6), Moses' brother, Aaron, participated in the disobedience of the people; Joshua did not. Joshua was waiting for Moses near the mountain of the Lord when he heard the noise of Israel's rebellion (Exodus 32:17).

In Exodus 33:11, Moses pitched a tent, known as the tent of meeting, outside the camp of Israel. It was in this tent that God met with Moses face to face. However, when Moses would leave the tent of meeting to return to the camp of Israel, Joshua, as Moses attendant, did not leave the tent. Joshua remained outside the camp in the place of the Presence. In this, we see that as a young man, Joshua learned the value of the Presence of the Lord.

As Joshua made his final address, he stood in the shadow of another choice made many years earlier at Kadesh Barnea. During the first encampment at Kadesh Barnea, as a nation, Israel rebelled against God and refused to enter the Promised Land, Canaan, for fear of giants seen in the land. But Joshua and Caleb, son of Jephunneh, exhorted people against rebellion and fear. They stood against the decision of the masses and encouraged Israel to fight (Numbers 14:6-9).

In this, Joshua demonstrated his choice to obey God, and he was resolute regardless of the decision of the nation. Joshua was unmoved by the decision of the assembly of Israel, even when the assembly considered stoning him along with Caleb. Joshua did not back up; he did not back down, and he did not give in to the opinion of the masses.

In these final words to Israel, at the age of 110, Joshua stood as living proof that his choice to serve the Lord was the right choice, regardless of the decision of the masses.

> Joshua's life was an example of the value of the personal choice to serve God, no matter what.

Have you made your choice to serve the Lord? If not, you can make that choice right now. Here's how:

> *The first step* is to enter into a relational conversation with God. That's what prayer is: talking to God and listening for His response.

Please understand that you don't have to be perfect to talk to God. God loves us so much that He sent His Son Jesus to make it possible for the ungodly to talk with God and become His child by faith.

> When we were utterly helpless, with no way of escape, Christ came at just the right time and died for us sinners who had no use for him.
>
> Romans 5:6, TLB
>
> As many as received Him, to them He gave the right to become children of God, to those who believe in His

name.

John 1:12

When you are ready to start a conversation with God, these are some words that might help you get started. Say these words out loud.

> Heavenly Father, according to your word in Jeremiah 29:11, you have a good plan for my life. Your word in Romans 3:23 says that we have all sinned and missed your plan. I need your help to find and follow your plan for my life.

Are there any specific actions or attitudes you need to ask God to forgive you for? If so, take a minute to ask God to forgive you for each. God's word says if we confess our sin, He, our God, forgives our sin and cleanse us, and we become right with Him (1 John 1:9).

Here are some words you can say if you aren't sure how to confess your sins:

> Father in Heaven, I confess to you that I have (specifically name an act you have committed, a sinful statement or lie you have spoken, or an evil thought or attitude you allowed to take root in your heart). Lord, I confess this sin and I ask you to forgive me and cleanse me from this sin, in Jesus' name, Amen.

Now go back and repeat this prayer for each sinful act,

statement or attitude that Holy Spirit brings to your mind.

When you are satisfied that you have asked forgiveness for all that Holy Spirit has brought to your attention, take time to thank Jesus for dying on the cross to make your forgiveness possible. Then, thank God for the Holy Spirit. Ask Holy Spirit to help you find and follow God's plan for your life (Ephesians 1:15-20).

If you followed these instructions, you have chosen Jesus as the Lord of your life. This is a decision to serve Him all the days of your life. You have made the right choice. You have made the best possible personal decision!

The following are some steps that you can take to prepare to more clearly hear the voice of Holy Spirit God's personal presence in you, as He begins to more clearly reveal His plan and purpose for your life.

1.   Set aside time every day to pray.

This is a time to talk with God as you would talk to any loving, caring person. Have faith that He hears you. The Holy Spirit is the presence of God living in your born-again spirit as a follower of Jesus, as one who has made Jesus Lord of your life. Talk with God, ask Him questions and take time to quiet yourself and listen. Be patient with both God and yourself. It may take some time for your spirit to get in tune with Holy Spirit and for you to begin to clearly discern His voice speaking to you.

As you purposefully and intentionally listen for God's voice, you will begin to recognize Holy Spirit speaking to you and in you. You will begin to recognize His voice over every other voice and thought that may be screaming for your attention.

Take time and make a place to engage God in intentional and personal conversation regularly, continuously.

2. Read the Bible.
If you don't know where to begin, start with the Gospel of John and Psalms. Prayer and Bible reading go hand-in-hand. Ask Holy Spirit to help you understand what you are reading and how it may apply to your daily life. The more familiar you become with the Bible, both Old and New Testaments, the more clearly you will understand what God is saying to you, the advice He is providing, the encouragement or correction He is giving and the good plan He is revealing for your life.

3. Don't keep your faith a secret.
Ask God to help you find a group of Bible believing, Jesus worshiping people who believe in the presence and power of Holy Spirit, a group that welcomes you to join them.
We all need alone time with God, but the New Testament describes believers as people who gathered and fellowshipped together, people who enjoyed spending time with each other. The believers described in the New Testament prayed for each other, worshipped together and helped each other grow in their understanding, faith and maturity as Christians. They became a household of faith. God's best plan for your future requires connection with others who share your faith in Jesus.

4. There is more!

Holy Spirit, God's presence in you as a believer, wants to fill every void in your life. He wants to fill you with dynamite power to overcome every obstacle in your path to His good plan for your life, to give you the tools, talents and gifts needed to succeed in all that God has prepared for you and your future. Read Acts, chapter 2, and ask God to fill you to overflowing with the person and power of the Holy Spirit. Ask and keep on asking Father God to fill you with Holy Spirit as often as you think of it until you know that you know beyond a shadow of a doubt the Holy Spirit fills your heart to overflowing, until the fruit of Holy Spirit (Galatians 5:22-25) and the gifts of Holy Spirit (1 Corinthians 12:1-11) are a living and real manifestation in your life.

God wants to talk with you much more than you can imagine. Here are a few additional suggestions and insights to help you on your journey with the Lord.

Asking God for forgiveness is not a "one and done" event.
In the future, Holy Spirit may bring to mind more specific things you will need to confess and ask God for His forgiveness. Do this as often as Holy Spirit keeps bringing things to your mind, even if it is multiple times per day. Holy Spirit wants to clean you up. As long as He keeps finding dirt, agree with Him, confess it and let it go down the drain like bath water.

Especially follow this pattern if you do or say something sinful after you have made Jesus the Lord of your life, whether your sins were done ignorantly or intentionally. Remember, it is never possible for you to want to be right with God more than He wants to be right with you.

The decision to follow Jesus you made today requires you to walk out your salvation day by day for every day of your life. Joshua's decision to worship the Lord was made long before his declaration in Joshua 24:15. Keep in mind; he had to walk it out day by day for over 40 years in the wilderness.

One key element of forgiveness remains, self-forgiveness.

The fact that you have confessed your sin and received God's forgiveness does not mean satan will not try to remind you of your past failure and inflict your spirit with depression and regret.

When this happens, remember that David moved on after repenting for the sins of adultery and murder (Psalm 51). He is included in the lineage of Jesus. Matthew refers to Jesus as the Son of David (Matthew 1:1).

Remember that before he became the Apostle Paul, Saul of Tarsus persecuted the Church (Acts 8:3) and was in consent to the stoning of Stephen (Acts 22:20). However, it is also the Apostle Paul who told the Philippian believers that he was focused on forgetting the past and pressing toward the promise of the future (Philippians 3:13). I strongly recommend that you do the same.

You have a destiny and an inheritance (Jeremiah 29:11; John 10:10). Like Joshua, it may have been delayed, but if you make the right choice, your God-ordained destiny and inheritance will be fulfilled. It will come at the appointed time (Habakkuk 2:3). Are you willing to serve the Lord regardless of what anyone else does or says?

As you press forward into God's plan for your

life, the good news is that Jesus has promised that He will never leave you. God is always with you (Matthew 28:20).

The importance of household choice, as for...my house.

As a direct bloodline descendant of Ephraim (1 Chronicles 7:20-27), Joshua spoke as an elder in the household of Ephraim. In the same sense, Joseph in the New Testament, was considered "the son of David" (Matthew 1:20), and Jesus "was of the house and lineage of David" (Luke 2:4) Joshua was the son of Ephraim. As such, Joshua was well within his authority to declare that his household, the household of Ephraim, would serve the Lord.

Why is this important today?

Believers have spiritual authority and accountability within their bloodline. Jesus made this point when He said, "No one can enter a strong man's house and plunder his goods, unless he first binds the strong man" (Mark 3:27).

From a biblical perspective, our goal is not just to be saved for our own personal or individual benefit. Our goal should be to stand strong in faith and intercession for our bloodline relationships, our household and extended family. When we make a personal decision to serve the Lord, we enter into God's plan to raise up men and women who understand their authority to stand as a spiritually strong one within their household.

As in the account of Cornelius and his household in Acts, chapter 10, and as in the account of the Philippian jailer in Acts 16:27-33, our personal decision can have powerful spiritual impact upon our household. Joshua's personal decision to serve the Lord, the strength of his personal faith and his position as an elder in the House of Ephraim empowered his decree, "My house will serve the Lord."

The value of national choice, choose yourselves.
In the final chapter of the Book of Joshua, he makes an impassioned farewell address to the assembly of the nation of Israel. His audience included the matteh, the tribal leaders of the bet or household of Israel, the descendants of Abraham, Isaac and Jacob. As a member of the tribe of Ephraim (Numbers 13:8), when Joshua uses the personal pronoun *you*, he is not only speaking as a leader to leaders; He is issuing an appeal to his bloodline relatives, his family, tribe and nation.

The heart of Joshua's charge to Israel as a nation is the exhortation to remain faithful to God who had faithfully fulfilled His promises to them (Joshua 23:14). In what resembles the renewal of wedding vows, Joshua calls upon the entire nation of Israel to renew their covenant to serve God, to serve Him alone and forsake all idol worship (Joshua 24:23-25).

In this, Joshua delivers a serious national warning. The leaders of Israel are put on notice that if they forsake the Lord and choose to serve foreign gods, disaster will come upon them and bring an end to Israel as a nation (Joshua 24:20).

Unfortunately, in the years to come, Israel's future generations did not heed Joshua's warning. Ultimately, Israel entered into periods of national idolatry. This idolatry resulted in its occupation by foreign invaders and its destruction. Because of their national disobedience, the people of Israel were forced to live in exile in the lands of their invading adversaries (2 Kings 17:1-41; 2 Chronicles 36:15-21).

Joshua's prophetic warning to Israel has been proven valid over many generations. During the time of Jesus, Israel was occupied and ruled by the Roman Empire. In this season, the importance and value of our decision to serve the Lord as a nation is as important to America today as it was to Israel as a nation in Joshua's day.

God is issuing a call to the United States of America and all the nations of Earth. It is a call to choose today whom you will serve.

Repeat after me.
Regardless of what this nation or any other nation may choose,

As for me and my house, We WILL serve the Lord!

CHAPTER 7

The Power of Parenting

> Train up a child in the way he should
> go [teaching him to seek God's
> wisdom and will for his abilities and
> talents], even when he is old he will
> not depart from it.
>
> Proverbs 22:6, AMP

Every generation has its unique challenges, issues and
temptations. Our grandparents never faced many of
the conflicting ideologies that confront us in the 21st
century. Given the pace of technological, social, moral
and political changes in this present era, how can we
possibly know how to prepare today's children for the
world of tomorrow?

First and foremost, the Bible places the
responsibility for preparing children for the future in
the hands of their parents. This intent is clearly
expressed in God's choice of Abraham to become the
father of a great nation (Genesis 18:18-19). Later, it is
expressed as a requirement of Old Testament Law
(Deuteronomy 6:6-9). In the New Testament, God's

intent is expressed in His choice of Mary and Joseph to serve as the parents of Jesus (Matthew 1:18-24; Luke 1:26-28).

The priesthood, the temple and the synagogue contributed to the training and development of Jesus during His childhood, adolescence and young adulthood. However, it was God's plan for the Redeemer of the world, the only begotten Son of God, to be nurtured and disciplined by parents in a household.

Holy Spirit is calling Christian parents everywhere to recover and reactivate this biblical pattern for raising children. Just as the household of Mary and Joseph was accountable to raise Jesus in a manner that would prepare him for His calling and destiny, today Holy Spirit is calling parents to prepare children to live out their heavenly calling and covenantal destiny. It is in the household that we should "train up a child."

> The teaching of the Scriptures is foundational to the issue of training up a child (Deuteronomy 6:6-9). Yet training up a child is more than legalistically teaching the letter of the Law. The letter of the Law produces death to the human spirit; the Spirit of the Law gives life and makes us spiritually alive (2 Corinthians 3:6).

As our children develop, we may not know every specific circumstance, issue or challenge they will face in the future. But we can let our intercessory prayers, loving nurture and godly instruction provide a blanket of protection around them in any stormy or turbulent situation they may experience. We can live before them as an illustration of the truth of Scripture in our daily walk with the Lord. We can clearly manifest the heart of God for our children. With godly and wise parents as role models, they will have an experiential frame of reference to guide them through repentance and restoration even when they become the victim of deception, perverted reasoning and the pressure to conform to the influence of the spirit of this age (Romans 12:2, Phillips New Testament of Modern English).

One of the best scriptural examples is found in the prodigal son parable (Luke 15:11-24). It is a well-liked teaching story, an earthly story with a heavenly meaning. At the beginning of Luke, chapter 15, a group of tax collectors and sinners drew near to Jesus to listen. A group of legalistic, religious critics, known as the Pharisees and scribes, also gathered around Jesus. The Pharisees and scribes objected to Jesus' hospitality toward the tax collectors and sinners, the religious outcasts of that time. To make matters worse in the eyes of the Pharisees and scribes, Jesus went so far as to eat with these outcasts.

The parable of the prodigal son is one of a series of parables that illustrate the value of lost things. It serves as Jesus' response to the criticism of the religious elitists and their attitude toward the tax collectors and sinners. The parable of the prodigal son is the account of a lost son.

In this story, the younger of two sons asked his father to give him his inheritance. In response to this request, the father divided up the substance of the estate between the sons. Shortly thereafter, with his inheritance in hand, the young man packed up his belongings and left for another country to live loose, wild and free from his father's supervision.

Boundaries

In his journey to a far country, the prodigal crossed some boundaries. Taken within the Jewish context of those to whom the teaching of this parable was directed, the prodigal's journey to reach a far country would have required him to cross his father's household boundaries, at least one tribal boundary, and at least one national boundary. Each one of these boundaries served to define the prodigal's place of provision, protection and identity. As he crossed these borders, the prodigal made an intentional choice to remove himself from their safety and security.

Not all the boundaries the prodigal crossed were visible. In his rebellion, the prodigal crossed some internal boundaries that had been established in his father's household. He crossed Spiritual and moral boundaries that were intended for his good.

Ultimately, as the result of foolish living and wasteful spending, hard times came upon the young man. When a famine came to this foreign land, he was devastated. With his money spent, the prodigal was forced to take a job feeding pigs. It is important to note that according to Jewish Law (Leviticus 11:7), pigs are unclean animals. Simply the smell of a pig farm is one of the foulest odors anyone could ever imagine. Feeding pigs was among the most despicable jobs a Jewish man could ever have.

In a far country, the prodigal had crossed the boundaries of moderation and morality (Luke 15:13, AMP). He found himself beyond the internal and external protection and provision he had known within the boundaries of his father's house, among his tribe and in his nation. The prodigal became so destitute and hungry that he considered eating the pods, carob beans, he was feeding to the pigs. No one offered to help him.

In this sad state of affairs, Scripture informs us that the prodigal finally began to understand life with his father was not so bad after all (Luke 15:17). The prodigal realized that he was in a crisis situation; he had hit rock bottom. He came face to face with the realization that he was in the wrong place doing the wrong thing.

When the prodigal hit rock bottom, he came to the place of repentance. In turning his life around, in changing his mind, he needed to know which way to turn. Scripture instructs us the goodness of God leads us to repentance (Romans 2:4). The kindness and goodness the young man observed in his father's life led him to change his mind (Luke 15:17-19). As his heart turned toward memories of home, he determined, "I will return to my father" (Luke 15:18). When the prodigal came to himself, he headed home.

The pain that the prodigal experienced in the far country was not his solitary pain. Godly parents of any age would agree that one of the most difficult, agonizing things a parent can endure is to watch their child go through the process of rebellion, bottoming out and entering recovery. As the prodigal made his way home, the father was eagerly awaiting his return. The father met his son with compassion and affection while he was still far from home. In retracing his steps back to his father, the prodigal found the restoration of identity, protection and provision. In his rebellion the prodigal had crossed multiple boundaries; in his returning, he discovered that he had never escaped the bounds of his father's love.

The father in this parable is Jesus'

characterization of the forgiveness and compassion of our Heavenly Father. This parable is a reminder that no matter how far from home or how deep in the muck and mire we find ourselves; He will never react in harshness or anger to our honest humility and true repentance (Psalm 51:17). To the Pharisees and scribes who heard Jesus tell this story, it was intended as a revelation of Heavenly Father's heart for the lost.

The Road Map Home

As a good Jewish father, the father in this parable would have provided his children with a proper Jewish upbringing in matters concerning the temple, the Law, priesthood and congregational worship. However, it was the Spirit of the Scriptures demonstrated by a godly parent in the context of household that became a beacon to light the path of restoration for the prodigal (Luke 15:17).

It is significant that the memories Jesus recounts as impactful to the repentance of the lost son were not religious memories. They were not his memories of lessons learned during times and events shared in the synagogue. They were not memories of the words and rituals of the religious leaders. The memories that guided the return of the prodigal were memories of his father in the context of the normal operation of his household. These memories were a potent lesson in godly living taught by the example set by a parent.

> How could you not know that His kindness is guiding our hearts to turn away from *distractions and habitual* sin to walk a new path?
>
> Romans 2:4, Voice

Scripture instructs parents to teach, nurture and discipline their children, but it is the behavior and attitudes that parents manifest in the daily circumstances and situations of life that speak loudest in preparing a child's heart. The living relational example of a godly parent forms the memories and values that a child can draw upon in the low seasons of life, times of despair, frustration and trouble. Scriptures quoted, sermons preached, and prayers prayed are significant to the spiritual development of any child. However, they become nothing more than a religious ritual, a façade, if we don't back it up with the daily demonstration of our Father's heart. His heart calls parents to a relationship of kindness and godliness, expressed by the fruit of the Spirit (Galatians 5:22-23) and illustrated in the father's life in the prodigal son parable.

Modern Prodigals
Many parents today wake up to suddenly find their child has crossed boundaries that have removed them from the protection and security of home. This parable illustrates the principal that even godly parents can raise up children who make bad decisions and sinful choices. The scriptural values and boundaries that parents have established in their household clearly and lovingly communicate and diligently demonstrate become most valuable in times like these.

The walls, boundaries and values of a place called home can seem like the confines of a prison to a child, especially to an adolescent or young adult, but in the dark, cold and stormy times of life, they provide protection, peace, security and comfort. Without the values of a godly home life, children, whether young or old, are left unprotected in a world of deception and danger. The limits we set for our children, the scriptural values we teach and reinforce by our example, the wise compassionate discipline we provide are the signposts that guide them back to safety when they become lost and far from home.

CHAPTER 8

The Power of Reconciliation

But also look ahead: I'm sending Elijah the prophet
to clear the way for the Big Day of God—the
decisive Judgment Day!

*He will convince parents to look after their
children and children to look up to their parents.*

If they refuse, I'll come and put the land under a
curse."
Malachi 4:5-6, MSG

It is important to understand that some who read this
may have never lived in a household of blessing or
experienced the kind and loving embrace of parental
forgiveness. Their story is about multiple generations
of prodigals, prodigal children as well as prodigal
parents caught in a self-perpetuating cycle of
dysfunction and trauma.

Children raised in a household caught in the
cycle of abuse, abandonment, neglect, addictive
behaviors, divorce or poverty are not likely to have a

healthy relational blueprint to draw from as they grow into adulthood and become parents themselves. As parents they cannot demonstrate or activate in their children what they were never taught or have never experienced in their own childhood.

This is a deceptive satanic cycle designed to persuade the generations of our bloodline to accept brokenness and iniquity as normal. It is a strategy that has embedded a root of bitterness and defilement into the lives of many (Hebrews 12:14-15).

How do prodigal parents establish generational blessing in their household and family when they have not received it from their mother or father? How will the children of dysfunction and abuse find salvation and relational wholeness when the only home they have ever known is defined by trauma and pain? How can we break the cycle of this multigenerational curse and establish generational blessing?

But God!

The Perfect Parent
Jesus is the perfect expression of God's intent, as a father who is a parent, toward His children (John 14:7-11). Jesus is the revelation of Our Heavenly Father as The Perfect Parent. Jesus came into the earth to reconcile the relationship between Father God and his prodigal children (John 1:12-13).

> All of this is *a gift* from *our Creator* God, who has *pursued us and* brought us into a restored *and healthy* relationship with Him through the

Anointed. And He has given us *the
same mission,* the ministry of
reconciliation, *to bring others back to
Him. It is central to our good news that*
God was in the Anointed making
things right between Himself and the
world. This means He does not hold
their sins against them. But it also
means He charges us to proclaim the
message that heals and restores our
broken relationships *with God and each
other.*

2 Corinthians 5:18-19, Voice

Though we may have never known the parental love
and forgiveness the prodigal son knew, Jesus has
given us the opportunity to know an even greater
dimension of parental loving kindness. He has made
it possible for each of us to become the spiritually
adopted children of our Heavenly Father (Romans
8:15-16). As we turn our hearts toward the Father, as
we seek reconciliation in our relationship with Him,
He will redeem our past. He will repay us for the lost
years we lived as prodigals (Joel 2:25). He will turn the
events and circumstances that were intended to harm
us into our personal blessing as well as blessing for
our household (Genesis 50:20).

As we experience Heavenly Father's pardon
from our transgressions, we are obligated to
demonstrate that same pardoning grace in every
relationship (Mark 11:26). In Christ, we are
commissioned and appointed to the ministry of
reconciliation. We are anointed and empowered by
Holy Spirit to provide the comfort we have received

to those in need of comfort (2 Corinthians 1:4). In our reconciliation to our Heavenly Father, we hear the call and find the grace to seek restoration in our household and family relationships.

It does not matter which generation we belong to or how old we are. Whether we are a parent, child or both, we who have been reconciled to God should seek reconciliation with all in our household and family. As a child, we need to turn our heart toward our parents. As a parent, we need to turn our heart toward our children. Our Perfect Parent loved us first. In this, as His children, we should follow His example; we should always be the first to love, always desiring and ministering reconciliation.

Dealing With Delay

Our reconciliation to Heavenly Father brings life to our hope for household reconciliation. However, reconciliation with others is not guaranteed. We may have waited for many years for the reconciliation of our prodigal relationships. We may have dreamed of what the day of restoration would be like. But, for some that day has not yet come.

When our dream of reconciliation faces the frustration of delay, we can find ourselves dealing with hope deferred, disappointment, even depression. When we find that we are in this place of discouragement, we should follow the example of David at Ziklag (1 Samuel 30:1-6). David faced the loss of his family and his earthly possessions at the hands of Amalekite raiders. He then faced the despair and frustration of his companions who had also experienced the loss of family and possessions. The distress of David's people became so intense they considered stoning him. But, David encouraged himself in the Lord.

> Why are you in despair, O my soul?
> Why have you become restless *and* disquieted within me?
> Hope in God *and* wait expectantly for Him, for I shall yet praise Him,
> The help of my countenance and my God.
>
> Psalm 42:11, AMP

Our peace and hope should not depend on the status of our relationship with any other human being. We should have godly hopes and expectations for our children, our parents, and our spouse. We should believe for our brothers and sisters in Christ to excel morally and spiritually. But, our peace and confidence should not depend upon any of them living up to our expectations. We should pursue peace, wholeness and reconciliation in every broken relationship, but our sense of well-being will find an immoveable foundation in the faith and expectation we place in God alone.

When our efforts toward reconciliation are rejected, it is important that we continue to intercede in prayer and possibly enter into a season of fasting as we continue to walk in faith believing reconciliation is possible. We should especially guard our heart against hope deferred and bitterness. We should continue to walk in the Spirit of reconciliation in the face of each and every rejection. Thankfully, our Heavenly Father did not give up on us. He continued to pursue reconciliation until we received His gracious offer.

> Let us not grow weary while doing
> good, for in due season we shall reap
> if we do not lose heart.
>
> Galatians 6:9

David encouraged himself in the Lord and recovered all (1 Samuel 30:18). He was reconciled to his family; his possessions were restored. It is in our relationship with Heavenly Father that we find the ability to deal with despair and delay. Reconciliation and recovery are God's good and perfect gifts (James 1:17) to those who make Him their hope, to those who walk as the reflection of His reconciling love. It is in seeking Father first that everything, including our relationships, is restored to their proper alignment and function in God's family plan.

Worst Case Scenario

> If it is within your power, make peace
> with all people.
>
> Romans 12:18, Voice

It is not always possible to make peace and find reconciliation in our family relationships. Not everyone in our household (parent or child) will understand their need to reconcile with us. Not everyone will be willing to receive our offer of reconciliation. We cannot violate another person's will, their right of choice.

Repentance and reconciliation go hand in hand. The prodigal son did not reconcile with his father until he "came to himself" (Luke 15:17). He changed his mind. Some are content to continue functioning in dysfunction. Some cling to bitterness and sin until their death. David's relationship with King Saul and his son Absalom illustrate this point.

Saul was a father figure to David. However, a spirit of jealousy drove Saul to threaten David's life. But instead of choosing to become bitter or to retaliate, David chose to respect the king and regard him with honor. When David realized that reconciliation with the king was impossible, he took the dramatic step of moving into the land of the Philistines, Israel's enemies, to escape Saul's repeated attempts to end his life (1 Samuel 27:1-4). Until his death, Saul refused to reconcile his relationship with David.

David's dearly loved son Absalom had allowed a great breach came into their relationship. Absalom set his heart to remove his father from the throne of Israel (2 Samuel 15:1-2). In the face of Absalom's plot of treason and treachery, David was forced to seek safety beyond the walls of Jerusalem (2 Samuel 15:13-14). As the result of a horrific accident, Absalom's life came to an end (2 Samuel 18:9-10). Absalom died without finding reconciliation with his father.

In these two examples from the life of David, neither Saul nor Absalom came to the place of repentance. Both Saul and Absalom died with bitterness embedded in their hearts. Neither Saul nor Absalom ever came to themselves.

Be Wise

> Therefore be wise as serpents and
> harmless as doves.
>
> Matthew 10:16

These examples from David's life also illustrate the wisdom of exercising caution when we discern that reconciliation is not an immediate option and we sense that we are in danger. David's example demonstrates there are situations and circumstances in which the best course of action is to remove ourselves from the presence of those who threaten our safety and well-being.

If anyone finds they are in an abusive relationship, it is advisable to seek the wisdom of an experienced and godly counselor. It may also be necessary to develop a safety plan, a strategy to implement when we need to remove ourselves from the threat of abuse or bodily harm. This is a worse case scenario, but it is reality for some.

Our Heavenly Father knows what it is like to love those who refuse the offer of forgiveness and reconciliation. Even though Jesus gave His life to make reconciliation possible, not everyone will choose to be reconciled to God. Many will choose to continue to live a life of sin and rebellion, refusing the gracious gift of God. But, that does not void the offer and possibility of reconciliation.

In our household and family relationships, we should not live in denial or danger when a barrier to reconciliation exists. However, we must make sure our heart is turned in the right direction. We must repent, change our mind and become willing to tear down any portion of any barrier that we have contributed to. From our side of the fence, the gate to the garden of reconciliation should always be open. But, those who are allowed to enter that garden must leave the poison of bitterness and hostility at the gate.

The Blessing of Reconciliation

Whether in the physical realm or in the realm of the Spirit, the powerful influence of godly parenting is a reflection of our Perfect Parent's desire to bring reconciliation into His relationship with and between His children. It is in this reconciliation that parents are given the opportunity to shape the godly destiny of their children and generations to come. Whether we have been a prodigal child, prodigal parent or both, reconciliation of all our generations is the longing of Father's heart.

As in the prodigal son parable, the reconciliation of relationship in both the natural and spiritual realm brings the restoration of blessing. But, reconciliation, restoration and blessing come with a condition, the condition that we turn, come to ourselves and begin the journey back to Father's presence.

When the heart of the parents return to the children and the heart of the children return to their parents the door is opened for multi-generational blessing to be established in our household, family, tribe and nation.

Reconciliation is an irreplaceable and powerful component of God's family plan.

CHAPTER 9

Bless the Children

I will praise You, for I am fearfully and
wonderfully made;
Marvelous are Your works,
And that my soul knows very well.
My frame was not hidden from You,
When I was made in secret,
And skillfully wrought in the lowest parts of
the earth.
Your eyes saw my substance, being yet
unformed.
And in Your book they all were written,
The days fashioned for me,
When as yet there were none of them.
Psalm 139:14-16

God knew you before you were born. He knew your child in the womb. As a mother or father, you should establish a relational bond of blessing with your child before he or she is born.

Before the birth of a child, pray earnestly asking God for His choice of a name. Throughout

Scripture, names have prophetic meaning. With the help of Holy Spirit, earnestly seek the right name for your child. Study the prophetic meaning of that name. Speak that name and its prophetic meaning over your child before and after birth, as often as the Holy Spirit reminds you. Don't just go with the current trendy names for children. Don't just automatically decide to name a child for a particular relative, sports hero or friend. The prophetic meaning of a name has a great influence upon their lives.

Ask God to give you a Bible verse that speaks prophetically to your child. Study the meaning of that verse and speak it over your child before and after birth as often as Holy Spirit reminds you. The verse spoken prophetically to children before birth can form a special spiritual bond between the parent, child and Scripture. This is an activity that best blesses your child when both parents are active in the process. Obviously, a child's mother has a 24/7 relationship with the baby during gestation, but the father should also speak into the child before birth. This is a unique time for spiritual bonding and blessing.

One of the foundational blessings parents should provide to their children, before or after birth, is to establish a physical and spiritual environment around them that offers security, happiness, peace and the opportunity to be at rest (Isaiah 32:18). Trauma, drama and chaos are detrimental to raising children in the nurture and admonition of the Lord. Establish an atmosphere of worship and praise around your child. Ask the Lord to establish your heart in peace and allow that peace to fill the atmosphere around your child.

Children were brought to Jesus so that
He might place His hands on them
[for a blessing] and pray.
　　　　　　　Matthew 19:13, AMP

It is commonly regarded that Matthew 19:13 is the
account of Jesus blessing children. However, the
words "bless" or "blessing" are not included in this
passage in most of the commonly read English
translations of the Bible. The Amplified Version
quoted above is one of the exceptions.

Most translations mention that children were
brought to Jesus for Him to lay his hands on them
and pray. The implication is that by placing His hands
on the children Jesus would impart a blessing to
them.

Another example of the blessing and power
of God manifested in an anointed touch is found in
the story of Ananias and Saul of Tarsus (Acts 9:17-
18). In this story Ananias placed his hands on the
blind eyes of Saul of Tarsus, which resulted in the
restoration of Saul's sight.

Again, the blessing of an anointed touch is
illustrated in the relationship between the Apostle
Paul and Timothy, his spiritual son (2 Timothy 1:6).
Paul laid his hands on Timothy and imparted a
spiritual gift. He blessed, added value and empowered
Timothy through the means of touch.

**Touch is one of the ways that godly
parents can bless their children.** The loving touch
of a parent has a powerful impact on almost every
aspect of a child's development. Holding hands, hugs
and tender loving pats are ways to express your heart

to a child.

Another way for parents to bless their children is by praying for them. As Jesus placed His hands on the children, He *prayed* for them. Following Jesus' example, parents should regularly pray a prayer of blessing over each child. This would be especially appropriate as children prepare for bed at night.

Yet, another way for parents to bless their children is to speak words of blessing over them. In the New Testament, the phrase "to bless" is "eulogeo," meaning "to speak well of."[1] This is the word used in Luke 24:50-51, as Jesus blessed[2] His followers before His ascension into heaven.

Eulogeo forms the basis for the English words eulogy and eulogize. Unfortunately, we tend to think of a eulogy as something that is read at a funeral when a person dies. Another meaning is a speech or a piece of writing in which you praise someone or something very much. From a biblical perspective, as it would apply to parents, blessing should be spoken over every child early and often.

Catch your child doing something good and complement them for it. Relationship is like a bucket, a blessing bucket. In a godly parent-child relationship more deposits should be deposited in your child's blessing bucket than withdrawals. To a child, discipline and correction may seem like a

---

[1] Vine, William Edwyn, Merrill Frederick Unger, and William White. Vines Expository Dictionary of Biblical Words. Nashville: T. Nelson, 1985. p69-70.
[2] Strong, James. *Strongs Exhaustive Concordance* Grand Rapids, MI: Baker Book House, 1983, G2127.

withdrawal from that bucket. Sometimes a small deposit can keep a child's blessing bucket from running dry.

The following are a few simple examples of things you can say, ask or do that may provide an opportunity to make some deposits in your child's blessing bucket.

- "Thank you for (specifically name something your child has done or said)."
- "I like the way you (specifically name something your child has done or said)."
- "What was the best, most interesting, or most exciting thing that happened to you today?"
- "Did God speak to you today?" "What did God say?"
- "What would you like to pray about?"
- "Who would you like to pray for?"
- "What did you dream about last night?"
- "What movie or TV show should we watch tonight?"
- "Can we go on a date (suggest a date and time?" If you know your child's favorite restaurant, park, sports activity, etc., you might suggest that. If not, you may need to ask, "Where would you like to go?"

Each child's personality, interests and aptitudes are different. Knowing yourself and your child well enough to recognize your similarities and differences will be a big help in knowing how to keep your child's blessing bucket full.

Listen to what Holy Spirit says about your

child. Holy Spirit knows more about your child than anyone. He knows best how to bless your child, your spouse and anyone else for that matter. But when it comes to keeping your child's blessing bucket full, no resource is as accurate and reliable as Holy Spirit.

Set aside a time once every week for household rest. Make this a special time to bless the children. Resting one day per week is God's idea (Genesis 2:1-3). Although Christians are not required to keep the Sabbath, a seventh day of rest, as a legalistic matter of the Law, we should remember that God established a day of rest long before the Law was established. We should also remember that Jesus is the Lord of the Sabbath (Matthew 12:8; Mark 2:28; Luke 6:5), and the Sabbath was made for our benefit (Mark 2:27).

One day per week, each household should set aside time for all its members to gather in the fellowship of rest. It should never be a foregone conclusion that every social, secular or school activity should take precedence over spending time together as a household. It is in this sense that the household is the Church and should not neglect coming together.

> Let us consider one another in order to stir up love and good works, not forsaking the assembling of ourselves together, as is the manner of some, but exhorting one another.
> Hebrews 10:24-25

A Word of Caution
This special time of blessing is a time of celebration, relaxation and fellowship, not a time to address

sensitive personal issues. Correction and discipline should be addressed privately on an individual case-by-case basis. This does not mean that issues that pertain to the entire household should not be discussed. It means that the focus should be on rest and relationship.

On whatever day of the week you and your household celebrate its day of rest, it should be a time to end an old cycle and enter into God's time of restoration for a new cycle ahead. Food, beverages and relaxing attire would be appropriate. This is not a formal event. It's about establishing a warm friendly, welcoming relational atmosphere. This gathering can be in the living room, around the pool, patio or even a campfire in the woods.

This might be a good time for parents and children to share what they have experienced in the preceding week, their accomplishments, activities, challenges, etc. Each family member should be given an opportunity to share. It can also be a time for each person to share the challenges and opportunities coming before him or her in the new week ahead.

Parents should take time to pray for each child. An opportunity should also be provided for each child to pray if he or she desires.

Parents should use this as an opportunity to pronounce a blessing over each child. A blessing should close the door on the week that has passed and open the door to God's grace, favor and success in the week ahead. When parents have concluded their words of blessing over each child, siblings may be invited to bless each other.

If you are unsure about how to go about blessing your children, the following words of blessing are adapted from the Aaronic Blessing found in Numbers 6:24-26. They are an example of words you can say.

> (Insert person's name) May you lay down the weight of any worry.
> From the week that is past and look to the week ahead
> With the expectation that the LORD will bless you
> And surround you with His protection.
> May the LORD'S presence be with you at all times;
> May the very thought of you put a smile upon God's face;
> May you always be aware of His love and kindness;
> May the LORD look upon you as one of His favorite children;
> May He give you a peaceful heart, a healthy body,
> A mind filled with wise thoughts and a mouth filled with words of faith to bless everyone you meet in this coming week.

When schedules become busy and hectic, you may choose a specific phrase of this blessing to speak over your child as a reminder, another deposit in their blessing bucket.

Bless your children by making praise and worship a part of your relationship with them. The joy of praise and worship should be something your children experience with you in the home. Your music and movement may not be perfect, but your heart to praise the Lord will bless your children. Get to know the style they prefer and join your children in their way of worshipping the Lord.

Keeping Your Bucket Full

As a parent, it will be difficult, if not impossible, to make deposits in your child's blessing bucket if yours is empty. How do you keep your blessing bucket full? The following are sources for parents to draw from to keep from running on empty:

Draw from your own personal relationship with the Lord. "Therefore with joy you will draw water from the wells of salvation" (Isaiah 12:3). If you don't know Jesus as your Savior, invite Him into your heart. Give Him control of your life today. If you have never developed a personal relationship with Jesus, I would encourage you to re-read chapter 6.

Be filled with the Holy Spirit (Acts 2:4). Holy Spirit has gifts to bring into your life that are indispensable to effective parenting. When you don't know what to do or say, let Holy Spirit be your teacher and guide.

Fill your mind and heart with God's Word. Regular Bible reading is a way to deposit the power of God's Word in your heart. The more Word you deposit in your heart, the more you will have to deposit in your child's blessing bucket.

A strong prayer life is another way to receive deposits in your personal blessing bucket. "Be anxious for nothing, but in everything by prayer and supplication, with thanksgiving, let your requests be made known to God" (Philippians 4:6).

Establishing an atmosphere and attitude of praise and worship is another source of deposits for your blessing bucket. Listen to praise and worship music in your home, in your car or wherever you are. Sing praises to the Lord. Don't wait to go to church to enjoy praise and worship.

> I will bless the Lord at all times; His praise *shall* continually *be* in my mouth.
>
> Psalm 34:1

A believing spouse is a blessing to draw from. Two parents standing in agreement with God and His word have great power with God (Matthew 18:19). Each parent should make deposits in their spouse's blessing bucket. You should speak blessing over each other as often as Holy Spirit brings it to mind. The sample blessing above is a good place to start.

Extended family can be a source of blessing. Relatives can be a source of blessing and assistance in the parenting process. If raised in a household of faith, extended family can be a very special blessing.

If extended family relationships have become strained or broken, ask God to minister healing to those hurts. Don't allow unforgiveness to stand between you and the blessing God wants to bring to the generations of your household.

Establishing a relationship with a congregation of believers that provides mentoring and support for parents is another source of personal blessing. You may be a single parent or no longer live near your parents or other relatives. If this is the case, congregational church as an extended family of faith should serve as a source for encouragement. These spiritual fathers, mothers, brothers and sisters in

Christ can be an irreplaceable source of deposits in your blessing bucket.

> Now my beloved ones, I have saved these most important truths for last: Be supernaturally infused with strength through your life-union with the Lord Jesus. Stand victorious with the force of his explosive power flowing in and through you.
>
> Ephesians 6:10, TPT

God has a plan to bless His children (Jeremiah 29:11). God has set an order and alignment in place to allow us the opportunity to both receive and distribute His blessing. In the beginning, He created Adam and Eve, male and female and set them together as a household. As man and wife they were commissioned to minister to all life on Planet Earth (Genesis 1:28). As His children, God blessed them with the ability and the authority to increase, multiply and to serve as stewards of His creation. Over the course of time, families, tribes and nations were formed as an outflow of the generations of the household of Adam and Eve.

Throughout history, God's family plan has continued to serve as a conduit of blessing. In the fullness of time, Jesus was born into the household of Mary and Joseph, another example of the importance of parents and household in God's plan for blessing humankind. In this modern era, our Heavenly Father is calling us to a new understanding of the importance of parents and households as His instruments of restoration and blessing for all times and seasons.

God's plan is for blessed parents to raise blessed children in households of blessing. It is in this pattern, according to God's family plan, that generational blessing will be established in the Earth.

> But for those who love Me and keep My directives, their children will experience My loyal love for a thousand generations.
>
> Exodus 20:6, Voice

DAVID AND KATHIE BURNETT

PART TWO

Emerging
Language, Literacy and Prophecy

Tools for Nurturing Very Young Children

Kathie Burnett

Emerging Language, Literacy and Prophecy

Tools for Nurturing Very Young Children

Chapter 1 – Tools of God's Nurturing Love and Gifts
1. God's Multigenerational Family System
2. Jesus Loves Children
3. Jesus Heals Children
4. Spiritual Gifts and Children
5. God Activates Training
6. All God's Children Have Been Given Spiritual Gifts
7. Spiritual Gifts and Me
8. Brown Bear, Brown Bear

Chapter 2 – Tools for Nurturing Parents and Developing Parenting Skills
1. Emerging Language, Literacy and Prophecy
2. Self-Care for Parents
3. Temperament
4. Goodness of Fit
5. Learning Modalities
6. Parenting Styles

Chapter 3 – Tools for Nurturing Language, Literacy and Prophecy
1. Emerging Language
2. Cycle of Learning Language
3. Emerging Literacy
4. Children's Literature

5. Emerging Prophecy
6. Prophets and Learning Modalities
7. Children's Literature and Prophecy
8. Jeremiah and the Visual Learning Style
9. Samuel and the Auditory Learning Style
10. David and the Kinesthetic-Tactile Learning Style

Chapter 4 – Tools of Nurturing Books and Activities
1. Children's Books with Spiritual Applications
2. A Word to Grandparents and Other Caregivers
3. Games, Activities, Experiences and Exploration
4. Safety
5. Ideas for Expanded Learning Activities
6. Book Sharing Tips

Chapter 5 – Final Thoughts about Nurturing
1. Final Thoughts about Caregiving
2. Your Destiny
3. A Word of Thanks

Appendix A - Resources for Parent Issues

Appendix B - Resources with Information about Childhood Issues

Authors' Pages
    Our Testimony
    Prayer of Blessing and Decrees for the Reader
    About the Authors

CHAPTER 1

Tools of God's Nurturing Love and Gifts

> Write these commandments that I've given you
> today on your hearts. Get them inside of you
> and then get them inside your children. Talk
> about them wherever you are, sitting at home or
> walking in the street; talk about them from the
> time you get up in the morning to when you fall
> into bed at night.
>
> Deuteronomy 6:7, MSG

God's Multigenerational Family System

Get ready for transition! Prepare for change! That's what Moses activated in Deuteronomy, chapters 5 and 6. He is equipping the Hebrew children to fulfill their destiny and enter into their Promised Land. He knows they will be moving on without his leadership. He needs to prepare and ready the people to keep going forward without him.

A brief look at this passage provides much insight. Moses reviews the Ten Commandments. Moses reminds the people of the greatest commandment, "You shall love the Lord Your God with all your heart, with all your soul, and with all your strength" (Deuteronomy 6:5). He is addressing the most vital principles of life that Father God has said must never be forgotten.

Moses clearly states that the foundational truths he is sharing are not just for the people that are present with him at that time. The words are for "you, your son and your grandson" (Deuteronomy 6:2). He emphasizes that thought when he says, "Get them inside of you and then get them inside your children" (Deuteronomy 6:7, MSG). Later when Moses references the land God promised, he says this is the land God swore to give "your fathers, to Abraham, Isaac and Jacob" (Deuteronomy 6:10).

Moses is instituting God's structure of faith that is to be established within families for three generations at a time. This tri-generational system involves one generation teaching the next generation with the wisdom and support of the previous generation. The pattern is to be repeated over and over again throughout all generations "that He might preserve us alive" (Deuteronomy 6:24).

Jesus loves children.

When He was on Earth, He didn't just love children from a distance. He invited them to come close, "I want little children to come to me." Scripture clearly expresses how Jesus feels about little ones. Let's take a look at what each of the Gospel writers has to say about Jesus and His interactions with children.

Matthew wrote:

> They brought little children to Jesus so that he would lay his hands on them, bless them, and pray for them. But the disciples scolded those who brought the children, saying, "Don't bother him with this now!"
>
> Jesus overheard them and said, "I want little children to come to me, so never interfere with them when they want to come, for heaven's kingdom realm is composed of beloved ones like these! Listen to this truth: No one will enter the kingdom realm of heaven

unless he becomes like one of these!"

Matthew 19:13-14, TPT

Mark records Jesus' attitudes and actions toward children.

> The parents kept bringing their little children to
> Jesus so that he would lay his hands on them
> and bless them. But the disciples kept rebuking
> and scolding the people for doing it. When Jesus
> saw what was happening, he became indignant
> with his disciples and said to them, "Let all the
> little children come to me and never hinder
> them! Don't you know that God's kingdom
> realm exists for such as these? Listen to the truth
> I speak: Whoever does not open their arms to
> receive God's kingdom like a teachable child will
> never enter it." Then he embraced each child,
> and laying his hands on them, he lovingly
> blessed each one.

Mark 10:13-16, TPT

Luke provides even more insight.

> The people brought their babies and small
> children to Jesus so that he might lay his hands
> on them to bless them. When the disciples saw
> this, they scolded the parents and told them to
> stop troubling the Master. But Jesus called for
> the parents, the children, and his disciples to
> come and listen to him. Then he told them,
> "Never hinder a child from coming to me. Let
> them all come, for God's kingdom realm
> belongs to them as much as it does to anyone
> else. They demonstrate to you what faith is all
> about. Learn this well: unless you receive the
> revelation of the kingdom realm the same way a
> little child receives it, you will never be able to

enter in."

Luke 18:15-17, TPT

John shares a demonstration of childlike faith and revelation of the Kingdom realm in his description of the story of feeding five thousand. This miracle is recorded in all of the Gospels (Matthew 14:13-21; Mark 6:30-44; Luke 9:10-17; John 6:5-13), but John includes some additional details.

As the story begins, thousands of men, women and children followed Jesus to an isolated place in the countryside. Scripture tells us people tracked Jesus everywhere He went because they had seen and heard about the miracles and healings that He ministered. They were in a remote location. It was late in the day. Jesus knew people were hungry and asked the disciples about food. Philip focused on lack and said they didn't have money to buy food for everyone. It seemed impossible.

Andrew noticed there was one child who was willing to share his lunch. Andrew didn't know what to do but he had learned enough to go to Jesus to tell Him about the child and what had been offered. Here's the story as written by John.

> Andrew, Simon Peter's brother, spoke up. "There's a young boy here with five barley loaves and two fish. But what good is that with this huge crowd?"
> "Tell everyone to sit down," Jesus ordered. So all of them—the men alone numbered five thousand—sat down on the grassy slopes. Then Jesus took the loaves, gave thanks to God, and passed them out to the people. Afterward he did the same with the fish. And they all ate until they were full. "Now gather the leftovers," Jesus told his disciples, "so that nothing is wasted." There were only five barley loaves to start with, but twelve baskets were filled with the pieces of bread the people did not eat!

> When the people saw this miraculous sign, they exclaimed, "Surely, he is the Prophet we have been expecting!"
>
> John 6:8-15, NLT

This was a miracle, as is said, of biblical proportions! Notice, that it was activated by a child. The child gave what he had even though it looked like a puny gift that was not enough to make any difference. By giving what he had, a child set this miracle in motion. Jesus received the offering and gave thanks for it. He touched and energized the gift transforming the totally impossible into the possible. Jesus took the offering of loaves and fish, multiplied it and the result was enough to feed the entire crowd with lots of leftovers.

Perhaps the child who so generously gave the food he had was blessed with leftovers to take home and share with his family. Most likely, this event significantly impacted that child. Maybe, because of what he learned from Jesus, he had faith to overcome lack for the rest of his life!

Much can be learned from this miracle. The importance of giving offerings including the value of giving thanks. The biblical principle of releasing faith and believing for Jesus to energize, activate and multiply one's gifts so that every need is met. And, of course, the biblical principle of demonstrating love for children just as Jesus did by respectfully honoring this little boy's faith and receiving what he had to offer. Remember, that a child led the way. It is written.

> A little child shall lead them.
>
> Isaiah 11:6, KJV

Jesus heals children.
Another way Jesus expressed His love for children was with miraculous healings. One example is the healing of a nobleman's son.

Jesus entered the village of Cana of Galilee where he had transformed water into wine. And there was a governmental official in Capernaum who had a son who was very sick and dying. When he heard that Jesus had left Judea and was staying in Cana of Galilee, he decided to make the journey to Cana. When he found Jesus he begged him, "You must come with me to Capernaum and heal my son!"

Jesus said to him, "You never believe unless you see signs and wonders."

But the man continued to plead, "You have to come with me to Capernaum before my little boy dies!"

Jesus looked him in the eyes and said, "Go back home now. I promise you, your son will live and not die."

The man believed in his heart the words of Jesus and set off for home. When he was still a distance from Capernaum, his servants met him on the road and told him the good news, "Your son is healed! He's alive!"

Overjoyed, the father asked his servants, "When did my son begin to recover?"

"Yesterday," they said, "at one in the afternoon. All at once his fever broke—and now he's well!"

John 4:46-52, TPT

Another example of Jesus' ministry to children is the healing of the daughter of Jairus. The account was written by Luke, the physician, in Luke 8 and also told in Matthew 9:18-26 and Mark 5:21-23.

When Jesus returned to Galilee, the crowds were overjoyed, for they had been waiting for him to arrive. Just then, a man named Jairus, the leader of the local Jewish congregation, fell before Jesus' feet. He desperately begged him to come and heal his twelve-year-old daughter, his only child, because she was at the point of death.

Jesus intended to go home with him but was surrounded by a large crowd including a woman who was desperate for healing.

Someone came from Jairus' house and told him, "There's no need to bother the Master any further. Your daughter has passed away. She's gone."

When Jesus heard this, he said, "Jairus, don't yield to your fear. Have faith in me and she will live again."

When they arrived at the house, Jesus allowed only Peter, John, and Jacob—along with the child's parents—to go inside. Jesus told those left outside, who were sobbing and wailing with grief, "Stop crying. She is not dead; she's just asleep and must be awakened."

They laughed at him, knowing for certain that she had died.

Jesus approached the body, took the girl by her hand, and called out with a loud voice, "My sleeping child, awake! Rise up!" Instantly her spirit returned to her body and she stood up.

Luke 8:40-56, TPT

It's important to recognize that Jesus love for children wasn't gender specific. He included girls as well as boys. Jesus is inclusive! Everyone has access to Him. His love is available to all, every female and male, adult and child, all people everywhere, people of every culture, every language, every tribe and every nation (Acts 17:26-27).

Spiritual Gifts and Children

> God's marvelous grace imparts to each one of us varying gifts and ministries that are uniquely ours.
>
> Romans 12: 6, TPT

Spiritual gifts are given to everyone. The Bible teaches that because of the marvelous grace of Father God through the sacrifice of Jesus by the power of the Holy Spirit all have been given spiritual gifts. All means each one. There are no age requirements or limitations in the Scriptures about receiving spiritual gifts. Children are definitely not excluded.

Certainly, the ongoing developmental process that children experience involves maturing in every area of life. Along with maturation in body, mind, will and emotions, spiritual growth and development is needed as well. This thought is described by the Apostle Paul.

> When I was a child, I talked like a child, I thought like a child, I reasoned like a child. When I became a man, I put the ways of childhood behind me.
>
> 1 Corinthians 13:11, NIV

> Beloved ones, don't remain as immature children in your reasoning ... but in your thinking be mature adults.
>
> 1 Corinthians 14:20, TPT

As their God-given gifts are identified, children need opportunities to receive instruction from someone who is more skilled and mature as well as opportunities to practice using their gifts in a safe environment. It is essential that children's spiritual gifts are nurtured in an atmosphere that allows them to blossom and develop. The same principle applies to adults. Adults can also grow and mature when they are given opportunities to cultivate and develop their spiritual gifts. According to 1 Corinthians 12, the entire Body of Christ benefits when the spiritual gifts of every believer are activated and operational.

Jeremiah is an example of a young person with an unknown spiritual gift that was identified and activated by Father God Himself. Here is Jeremiah's account of what happened.

> The words of Jeremiah son of Hilkiah, one of the priests at Anathoth in the territory of Benjamin. The word of the LORD came to him in the thirteenth year of the reign of Josiah son of Amon king of Judah, and through the reign of Jehoiakim son of Josiah king of Judah, down to the fifth month of the eleventh year of Zedekiah son of Josiah king of Judah, when the people of Jerusalem went into exile.
>
> The word of the LORD came to me, saying,
>
> "Before I formed you in the womb I knew you, before you were born I set you apart; I appointed you as a prophet to the nations."
>
> "Ah, Sovereign LORD," I said, "I do not know how to speak; I am only a child."
>
> But the LORD said to me, "Do not say, 'I am only a child.' You must go to everyone I send you to and say whatever I command you. Do not be afraid of them, for I am with you and will rescue you," declares the LORD.
>
> Then the LORD reached out his hand and touched my mouth and said to me, "Now, I have put my words in your mouth. See, today I appoint you over nations and kingdoms to uproot and tear down, to destroy and overthrow, to build and to plant."

Jeremiah 1:1-11, NIV

Jeremiah had a God encounter. Revelation after revelation was released. God said He knew Jeremiah before he was born on Earth. God revealed that He designed, fashioned and formed Jeremiah. God told Jeremiah that he was created, chosen, and set apart to be His mouthpiece, a spokesperson of Almighty God. What an amazing word!

Jeremiah's response was not so amazing. He offered God excuses based upon fear. Jeremiah said, "I'm just a child. I'm too young. I can't speak." Those words may sound familiar. Sometimes when a God-inspired word comes from Heaven, the human response is to try and clarify the situation in an attempt to help God fully understand. Those earthly explanations often begin with phrases like "I'm just..." or "I'm too..." or "I can't....."

The good news is that Father God saw past Jeremiah's excuses and looked deeper into the heart of the matter. He recognized that Jeremiah was afraid. He knew that Jeremiah had a root fear of people. Father understood that Jeremiah was afraid of how people might look at him, what they might say about him and even what they might do to him.

Father reassured Jeremiah. He promised to always be with Jeremiah and never abandon him. A similar thought is expressed in Hebrews.

> I will never leave you alone, never! And I will
> not loosen my grip on your life!
> Hebrews 13:5, TPT

Father God went on to promise He would protect, defend, deliver, preserve and rescue Jeremiah. Along with those words of reassurance, God also touched Jeremiah. Father God, God of the Universe, Ancient of Days, reached down, placed His finger on Jeremiah's mouth and said He would fill his mouth with words so potent that they would have a tremendous impact when spoken by Jeremiah at the right time, in the right place and expressed the right way. God promised when Jeremiah released God's targeted words, powerful messages would be communicated to nations and kingdoms. Those messages would be infused with the purposes of the Kingdom of Heaven and be capable of destroying, breaking down, building up and planting. God's words spoken from Jeremiah's mouth would activate global change and transformation. Literally, Jeremiah would release the authority of Almighty God through words with power to change the world!

God Activates Training

After Father God appointed and anointed Jeremiah for his God-given calling, God's next step was to begin the training process. To activate and acclimate Jeremiah as a prophet, God used an on-the-job method of training. He initiated training by simply asking Jeremiah a question and waiting to hear Jeremiah's response.

> The word of the LORD came to me: "What do you see, Jeremiah?"
> "I see the branch of an almond tree," I replied.
> Jeremiah 1:11

Apparently, answering this question was easy for Jeremiah. All he had to do was just report what he saw. God must have gifted him to be able to see into another realm so he could see what God asked him to see. When Jeremiah said he saw an almond tree, God immediately confirmed that Jeremiah's answer was correct. God continued the training session by sharing insight and explaining multilevel understanding about what seeing that almond tree meant. God taught Jeremiah by making clear that the vision of an ordinary almond tree was filled with an extraordinary message.

God repeated the training process by asking Jeremiah the same question again in Jeremiah 1:13, *What do you see?* And again, Jeremiah was able to respond with no difficulty. God continued the practice session by explaining the multidimensional message embedded in the picture Jeremiah saw.

Notice Father God's training system gives Jeremiah opportunities to practice the skills needed by a prophet while in the safety of His Presence and away from critical eyes of others. Father God never sets His children up for failure. He always offers an opportunity to learn that results in a set-up for success.

The question *What do you see?* seems to be one of Father God's favorite techniques for teaching, training and communicating with His prophets. That question is repeated three times in the book of Jeremiah, twice in Amos and two more times in Zechariah.

> Moreover, the word of the LORD came to me, saying, "Jeremiah, what do you see?"
> And I said, "I see a branch of an almond tree."
>
> Jeremiah 1:11

> The word of the LORD came to me the second time, saying, "What do you see?"
> And I said, "I see a boiling pot, and it is facing away from the north."
>
> Jeremiah 1:13

> Then the LORD said to me, "What do you see, Jeremiah?"
> And I said, "Figs, the good figs, very good; and the bad, very bad, which cannot be eaten, they are so bad."
>
> Jeremiah 24:3

> And the LORD said to me, "Amos, what do you see?"
> And I said, "A plumb line."
> Then the Lord said: "Behold, I am setting a

plumb line
In the midst of My people Israel; I will not pass
by them anymore."

Amos 7:8

And He said, "Amos, what do you see?"
So, I said, "A basket of summer fruit."
Then the LORD said to me: "The end has come
upon My people Israel; I will not pass by
them anymore."

Amos 8:2

And he said to me, "What do you see?"
So I said, "I am looking, and there is a
lampstand of solid gold with a bowl on top of it,
and on the stand seven lamps with seven pipes
to the seven lamps."

Zechariah 4:2

And he said to me, "What do you see?"
So I answered, "I see a flying scroll. Its length is
twenty cubits and its width ten cubits."

Zechariah 5:2

God asked His prophets the same question at least seven
different times in Scripture. Whenever God speaks, it is
important to listen, but when He repeats Himself over and over
again, it is absolutely noteworthy. Time and again, God used the
same question to initiate and activate His prophets. This biblical
pattern is a teaching technique that was used by Father God to
train His prophets. Godly visitations and prophetic training
frequently began by simply asking, *What do you see?*

All God's children have been given spiritual gifts.
Jeremiah was gifted by God to be an appointed spokesperson in
a specific time at a specific place. Certainly, no one else has ever
been anointed and appointed in the exact same way. But

117

Scripture tells us that all have been given gifts.

> Every believer has received grace gifts, so use
> them to serve one another as faithful stewards of
> the many-colored tapestry of God's grace.
>
> 1 Peter 4:10, TPT

Just as each individual has been uniquely created, each one has also been uniquely gifted. Father God has graced all His children with gifts. The Bible says that spiritual gifts are for everyone.

It is impossible to develop insight about spiritual gifts without considering the Source of the gifts. Meditate for a minute on the multidimensional, magnificence of God. Reflect on His creativity, originality, innovation and imagination. Think about the depth of His compassion and His limitless wisdom. Then begin to comprehend that He is the Giver who so generously and graciously gives gifts to all!

Spiritual gifts reflect the nature of their Source. They are varied and have different expressions and purposes. They are multidimensional. Scripture provides three separate groups of spiritual gifts that can be labeled as motivational, ministry and office gifts.[1]

Motivational Gifts

> We have different gifts, according to the grace
> given to each of us. If your gift is prophesying,
> then prophesy in accordance with you faith; if it
> is serving, then serve; if it is teaching, then teach;
> if it is to encourage, then give encouragement; if
> it is giving, then give generously; if it is to lead,
> do it diligently; if it is to show mercy, do it
> cheerfully.
>
> Romans 12:6-8, NIV

---

[1] Dr. Robert Heidler, Spiritual Gifts, message delivered at Glory of Zion International, November 18, 2018.

Ministry Gifts

Each believer has received a gift that manifests the Spirit's power and presence. That gift is given for the good of the whole community. The Spirit gives one person a word of wisdom, but to the next person the same Spirit gives a word of knowledge. Another will receive the gift of faith by the same Spirit, and still another gifts of healing—all from the one Spirit. One person is enabled by the Spirit to perform miracles, another to prophesy, while another is enabled to distinguish those prophetic spirits. The next one speaks in various kinds of unknown languages, while another is able to interpret those languages. One Spirit works all these things in each of them individually as He sees fit.

1 Corinthians 12:7-11, Voice

Office Gifts, Positions of Authority

He has appointed some with grace to be apostles, and some with grace to be prophets, and some with grace to be evangelists, and some with grace to be pastors and some with grace to be teachers. And their calling is to nurture and prepare all the holy believers to do their own works of ministry, and as they do this they will enlarge and build up the body of Christ.

Ephesians 4:11-12, TPT

There is great diversity and variety in the expression of thespiritual gifts. Since each individual believer is a unique creation, the way the gifts are released can also be unique. Gifts must be used in submission to and alignment with spiritual authority. Accountability is necessary because the overall purpose of spiritual gifts is to benefit the Body of Believers.

Spiritual Gifts and Me

After learning about spiritual gifts, and sometimes even before, most Christian believers begin to ask God about their own gifts and callings. This is often a process that continues throughout life. As relationship with Father God, the Lord Jesus and Holy Spirit deepens, so does revelation and understanding. The result is often an even greater anointing and activation of spiritual gifts.

Along the journey of seeking Father's heart for my own life, there is one verse that Holy Spirit highlighted or "lit up" for me.

> Follow the way of love and eagerly desire spiritual gifts, especially the gift of prophecy.
> 1 Corinthians 14:1, NIV

Since childhood, choosing the way of love has been foundational. That means love has been a priority even though I often fall short, and there is much, much more to learn and express. For years, I have known that spiritual gifts were God-given and had to be stewarded and developed. But the idea of pursuing spiritual gifts in the way described in this verse was somewhat of a novel thought.

The Greek word for "desire" used in this passage means "zealous" or "to covet." It means "to have warmth of feeling for or against."[1] That's interesting. Folks do seem to have strong feelings about spiritual gifts. Sometimes they are strongly for and sometimes they are strongly against. There seem particularly strong emotions about the gift of prophecy.

Since Scripture instructs us to desire spiritual gifts, I purposed in my heart to learn more, especially about prophecy. I asked God to teach me and even began to consider the possibility of being able to prophesy myself. One basic step in

---

[1] Biblesoft's New Exhaustive Strong's Numbers and Concordance with Expanded Greek-Hebrew Dictionary. (Biblesoft, Inc. and International Bible Translators, Inc., 1994, 2003); desire; NT:2206.

this process was to define prophecy.

In their book, *When God Speaks*, Chuck D. Pierce and Rebecca Systema Wagner share the following definition of prophecy.[1]

> The definition of "prophecy" is simple. Prophecy is speaking the mind and heart of God as revealed by the Holy Spirit. Prophecy is the outflow of the heart and very nature of God. Revelation 19:10 says that the testimony of Jesus is the spirit of prophecy. Jesus cares about His Church and therefore, has things He wants to communicate to His Church. Those communications come by way of the Holy Spirit. That is prophecy. It is what Jesus is saying to His Church.
>
> The testimony of Jesus, which is prophecy, is not just a corporate promise. Jesus says that His sheep know His voice (John 10:4). If you are one of His sheep, you have the capability, the capacity and the privilege of hearing the voice of your Shepherd that comes through the Holy Spirit.

As I continued to grow in understanding and faith, my desire also grew. I boldly asked Father God to give me a word of prophecy. And one day, He did. I was at home on an ordinary day doing everyday things when He spoke.

Holy Spirit dropped four words into my spirit. My first response was to laugh. Those words were not what I expected! Immediately, the words exploded inside me downloading the

---

[1] Chuck D. Pierce with Rebecca Wagner Systema, *When God Speaks*, (Bloomington, Minnesota: Chosen Books; 2005), 21 and Chuck D. Pierce with Rebecca Wagner Systema, *The Spiritual Warfare Workbook*; Chuck D. Pierce with Rebecca Wagner Systema, (Bloomington, Minnesota: Chosen Books; 2016), 29.

entire message that was contained in them. Much of this book is about sharing the message that was embedded in those four words.

Brown Bear, Brown Bear

Here they are, the four words Holy Spirit spoke to me: *Brown Bear, Brown Bear.*

Brown Bear, Brown Bear, What Do You See?[1] is one of the most beloved children's books of all times. Written by Bill Martin, Jr. and illustrated by Eric Carle, it was first published in 1967. Born in Hiawatha, Kansas in 1916, Bill learned the love of language from his grandmother. She shared tales about the family's history that became Bill's first lessons in storytelling.[2] Even though Bill's grandmother had only three months of formal schooling, she was an avid reader. Although Bill shared a growing love of oral language with his grandmother, he had difficulty reading as a child. Mr. Martin was in college before he read an entire book for the first time. While at Emporia State University, Bill discovered he could develop his reading skills by memorizing poems. The rhythm, rhyme and lyrical, even musical, nature of the poetry helped him identify words on the printed page.[3]

Later, Mr. Martin applied his own learning experiences to the books he wrote for preschoolers. During his lifetime, he wrote over 300 children's books. His other careers included serving as a teacher, principal, textbook editor and educational

---

[1] Bill Martin, Jr., *Brown Bear, Brown Bear, What Do You See?* (New York, NY: Holt, Rinehart and Winston; Renewed 1996; First Published: 1967; First Board Book Edition Published: 1996).

[2] Encyclopedia.com, Children's Literature Review (2009), *Bill Martin, Jr. 1916-*, https://www.encyclopedia.com/children/academic-and-educational-journals/bill-martin-jr-1916. Accessed 9/15/2019.

[3] Reading Rockets, *Transcript from an interview with Bill Martin Jr.* https://www.readingrockets.org/books/interviews/martin/transcript. Accessed 9/15/2019.

innovator. He achieved all these accomplishments even though his reading skills were not fully developed until he was in college.[1]

Brown Bear, Brown Bear is a simple picture book that was designed to help young children learn to identify colors and animals as well as motivate and encourage them to read. It uses rhythm, rhyme and repetition to quickly engage children and give them opportunities to read along. Because of its style and structure, children are usually able to go through the entire book in a single setting, often on their first try. This success develops a "can do" attitude and builds in children a confidence in their ability to read. The book also has a playful sense of adventure that is just plain fun!

Throughout the book, each animal, along with the children and teacher, are all asked the same question, *"What do you see?"* The response is always *"I see a ...looking at me,"* and, with the turn of the page, the next animal is named. The text follows this pattern: brown bear sees a red bird; red bird sees a yellow duck; yellow duck sees a blue horse; blue horse sees a green frog; green frog sees a purple cat; purple cat sees a white dog; white dog sees a black sheep; black sheep sees a goldfish; goldfish sees the teacher; the teacher sees the children and the pattern continues.

Focus on the simple question that is asked over and over again, *"What do you see?"* That is what Holy Spirit quickened to me. This favorite children's book is also a book of Scripture verses. On page after page, it asks the exact same question that Father God used to train some of His most important prophets.

In board book form, *Brown Bear, Brown Bear[1]* is

---

[1] Eden Ross Lipson, *Bill Martin Jr., 88, Reading Expert Who Drew on His Own Experience*; (New York Times, Aug. 14, 2004) https://www.nytimes.com/2004/08/14/arts/bill-martin-jr-88-reading-expert-who-drew-on-his-own-experience.html. Accessed November 21, 2018.

appropriate for toddlers as well as preschoolers. Caregivers can also read it to infants and even unborn babies. Holy Spirit revealed that the development of prophetic skills can begin very early, with the very young, in relationship-based interactions that are delightful fun for everyone!

[1] Bill Martin, Jr., *Brown Bear, Brown Bear, What Do You See?* (New York, NY: Holt, Rinehart and Winston; Renewed 1996; First Published: 1967; First Board Book Edition Published: 1996).

CHAPTER 2

Tools for Nurturing Parents and Developing Parenting Skills

Emerging Language, Literacy and Prophecy

Think about a newborn baby. At birth, every baby is helpless, completely dependent on caregivers. The only form of communication a baby has is crying. With that first cry, the baby is announcing, "I'm here! Take care of me!" The baby can't walk or talk or take care of its basic needs. It's the responsibility and, hopefully great joy of parents, family members and other caregivers to meet those needs.

Baby's needs include feeding, changing diapers and a place for safe sleep. There are other needs as well. The first few years of life are a time of amazing brain development and growth in every domain including cognitive (learning, thinking; problem-solving); language and communication; social and emotional; movement and physical development.[1]

In order to thrive, all young children need safe, stable, nurturing relationships and environments.[2] The consequences

---

[1] Centers for Disease Control and Prevention (CDC), *Developmental Milestones*, https://www.cdc.gov/ncbddd/actearly/milestones/index.html. Accessed 9/15/2019.
[2] Centers for Disease Control and Prevention (CDC), *Essentials for Childhood, Steps to Create Safe, Stable, Nurturing Relationships and Environment*, https://www.cdc.gov/violenceprevention/childabuseandneglect/essentials.html. Accessed 9/15/2019.

of not providing this kind of environment have been well documented. Studies conducted by René Spitz in the 1940s[1] and Harry Harlow in the 1960s as well as the research about Romanian orphans[2] that was authored by Nathan Fox in the 1990s all confirmed that healthy child development is only possible in a climate that is rich in human contact and social interaction. Their findings provide evidence that early childhood relationships and experiences have a powerful impact on growth and brain development.

Childhood trauma can also have a powerful impact on health and behavior throughout life. This was extensively researched and documented in the Adverse Childhood Experiences (ACE) Studies conducted by Vincent Felitti, head of Kaiser Permanente's Department of Preventive Medicine, and Robert Anda from the Centers for Disease Control and Prevention (CDC).[3] The initial ACE Study was conducted from 1995 to 1997 with over 17,000 participants that had the following demographics: about half were female; 74.8% were white; the average age was 57; 75.2% had attended college; all had jobs and were in good health.

The researchers identified a total of 10 types of Adverse Childhood Experiences (ACEs) that were categorized into three groups: abuse, family or household challenges and neglect. The three types of abuse included: sexual, verbal and physical. The five types of family dysfunction included: mental illness in the household, mother treated violently, household substance

---

[1] *History Module: The Devastating Effects of Isolation on Social Behaviour*, http://thebrain.mcgill.ca/flash/capsules/histoire_bleu06.html. Accessed 9/15/2019.
[2] Stephanie Pappas, Live Science Contributor, Life Science, *Early Neglect Alters Kids' Brains*, July 23, 2012, https://www.livescience.com/21778-early-neglect-alters-kids-brains.html. Accessed 9/15/2019.
[3] Centers for Disease Control and Prevention (CDC), *Adverse Childhood Experiences (ACEs)*, https://www.cdc.gov/violenceprevention/childabuseandneglect/acestudy Accessed 9/15/2019.

abuse, parental separation or divorce and incarcerated household member. Later, emotional and physical neglect were added.

Results of the study found that almost two-thirds of the participants reported having at least one Adverse Childhood Experience (ACE) and more than twenty percent reported experiencing three or more ACEs. Cumulative childhood stress was assessed based on the ACE score or the total sum of different categories of ACEs reported by participants. The study revealed that as the ACE score increased the potential for negative health and negative well-being outcomes also increased.[1] In other words, there is a direct link between childhood trauma and adult onset of chronic disease, mental health issues and behavioral problems.

The higher the number of ACEs, the greater the risk for the following: alcoholism and alcohol abuse; chronic obstructive pulmonary disease; depression; fetal death; health-related quality of life; illicit drug use; ischemic heart disease; liver disease; poor work performance, financial stress; risk for intimate partner violence; multiple sexual partners; sexually transmitted diseases; smoking; suicide attempts; unintended pregnancies; early initiation of smoking; early initiation of sexual activity; adolescent pregnancy; risk for sexual violence; poor academic achievement.

The major findings of the ACE studies revealed that ACEs are common among all sectors of society. Further, it is not uncommon for people who report a single ACE to experience adversity in additional ACE categories. Finally, there is often a direct relationship between negative childhood experiences and major risk factors for the leading causes of illness, death and poor quality of life among adults.

---

[1] Jane Ellen Stevens, *The Adverse Childhood Experiences Study — the largest, most important public health study you never heard of — began in an obesity clinic,* ACES Too High News, October 3, 2012, https://acestoohigh.com/2012/10/03/the-adverse-childhood-experiences-study-the-largest-most-important-public-health-study-you-never-heard-of-began-in-an-obesity-clinic. Accessed 9/15/2019.

The ACE study outcomes resulted in an increased social awareness of the potential lifelong impact of childhood trauma. Practices, programs and policies have been influenced by ACE research. A number of disciplines including education, criminal justice, healthcare, mental health, public health, workplace, and faith-based have developed systems of trauma-informed care. Child advocacy and prevention programs have been established with the purpose of putting a stop to ongoing generational trauma.

Resources that activate protective factors like the Strengthening Families Protective Factors Framework[1] can help overcome the negative impact of trauma. The Protective Factors Framework is a research-informed approach to increase family strengths and build key protective factors that enable children to thrive. The five protective factors that form the foundation of strengthening families are parental resilience, social connections, knowledge of parenting and child development, concrete support in times of need, and social and emotional competence of children. These core attributes are easy to understand and recognize. The protective factors support families as they successfully navigate the difficult situations of life.

Risk does not determine destiny. Awareness and healing intervention can lead to positive changes and healthier outcomes.

Trauma can seriously impact relationships. Issues like parental mental health, substance abuse and interpersonal violence can be extremely challenging for children as well as adults. Maternal depression, for example, often interferes with the developing relationship between a mother and child. These and similar issues should not be ignored and need to be addressed by professionals or those with special training. Some

---

[1] Center for the Study of Social Policy, *Strengthening Families and the Protective Factors Framework*, https://cssp.org/resource/about-strengthening-families-and-the-protective-factors-framework. Accessed 9/15/2019.

online resources that might be helpful are included in the Appendix A of this book. It is important to recognize that online resources can quickly become outdated, inaccurate or unavailable because of new research and other issues. If needed, readers are encouraged to reach out and find help in the local community.

Self-Care for Parents

Becoming a parent is a major life transition that comes with many changes including some that are quite unexpected. Change is challenging for almost everyone. Learning more about parenthood is one way to begin to address the challenges. Discovering new skills to address childhood issues and learning parenting tips can be helpful ways to reduce the stress of parenting. A multitude of parenting handbooks are readily available as well as a number of online resources some of which are listed in the Appendix B of this book. Most communities offer local parenting resources as well. Information about caring for infants, toddlers and children is necessary, but parents also need to consider how to meet their own needs in the midst of the caregiving they do for others.

Think about traveling on an airplane. The flight attendant always announces that, if the oxygen masks drop down, caregivers should put on their own masks first, and then help the children with their masks. In this situation, as in all of life, both the child and the adult need care. Children have many needs that must be met. In order to have the energy to meet those needs, parents need to make sure their basic needs are also met.

Self-care includes taking care of oneself by providing many of the same things that parents provide for their children. For every parent, simple things like getting enough sleep and eating healthy meals are necessary but all too easily neglected. Of course, parents have other needs that should be addressed, too. The key to self-care is to develop a balanced life based on personal priorities. Top priority is caring for one's children with a goal of nurturing and preparing them for life. Along with that, each caregiver can choose their own list of important priorities. The next step might be to plan what can be done to ensure those priorities become part of one's lifestyle.

The list will be different for each individual but will generally include items from these categories: emotional, social, psychological, creative/artistic and spiritual. Here is a list of each category to consider.[1]

Physical self-care can include:
- Eating a healthy diet.
- Getting enough exercise.
- Receiving regular, preventive medical care.
- Establishing a routine for sufficient sleep.
- Getting time away from the phone, email, TV and social media.
- Spending time in fresh air and natural light.

Emotional/Social/Psychological self-care can include:
- Enjoying and working on their marriage or other relationships.
- Spending time with friends and family.
- Staying in touch with other people.
- Expressing emotions, allowing yourself to cry and finding things that make you happy.
- Reading.
- Getting a massage or going to a spa.
- Reducing stress.
- Saying no to extra responsibilities.

Artistic/Creative/Spiritual self-care can include:
- Giving yourself quiet time for self-reflection.

[1] Program for Early Parent Support (PEPS), *Self-Care for Parents*, http://www.peps.org/ParentResources/by-topic/self-care/self-care-for-parents. Accessed 9/15/2019.

- Attending a local place of worship.
- Writing in a journal.
- Spending time out in nature.
- Enjoying a hobby or trying something new.

New parents sometimes need to ask for help. Taking a long nap or a hot bath while a trusted caregiver watches baby can make a big difference. Sometimes more help is needed. Primary caregivers are especially encouraged to recognize their own personal needs and identify sources of support.

When day-to-day activities and the necessities of life become wearisome and even overwhelming, it can be helpful to make a list of stressors. Write down those little things that are very frustrating along with major life stressors. Being aware of personal limits is important for self-care. Consider highlighting two or three stressful things and then think about a single action-step that may help relieve that specific stress.

Make a list of stress relievers. The list can include hopes for major life dreams and experiences. Perhaps even more important is making a list of those little things that help one get through the day with a smile. Consider ways to include one or two of those stress relievers in the daily schedule. Nurture your self-care every day by remembering to speak gratitude, bless loved ones and be kind to yourself!

Temperament
Differences in child development are not only impacted by the environmental influences in each child's life but by individual differences within each child as well. Children are born with differing temperaments, learning styles, physical characteristics and preferences. In other words, child development is not just impacted by the child's caregiving environment but also by the child's own nature. A comprehensive perspective of child development includes an understanding of the interaction between the child's nature and the impact of the environmental nurturing the child has received. Child development is a matter

of how the child's nature is nurtured.

Temperament refers to an individual's behavioral style and characteristic way of responding to situations including expression and regulation of emotions. Temperament tends to be consistent and is usually considered to be biologically based making it relatively independent of environmental influences.[1]

In the 1960s, Thomas and Chess initiated their classic longitudinal study of temperament that was conducted over three decades and followed babies from the age of three months to adulthood. The researchers studied nine characteristics of temperament including activity level, rhythmicity or regularity, distractibility, approach or withdrawal response to new situations, adaptability, attention span and persistence, intensity of reaction, sensitivity, and quality of mood.[2] The results of the study identified three basic types or clusters of temperament that the original researchers labeled easy, difficult and slow-to-warm-up.[3,4]

Children with an easy temperament establish consistent routines for activities like sleeping and eating, have mild reactions and are usually in a positive mood. They tend to approach and adapt to new situations easily. Approximately

---

[1] PsychPage... perspectives on psychology in daily life, *Temperament and Development, Child Temperament—based on Thomas & Chess, 1977,* http://www.psychpage.com/family/library/temperm.htm. Accessed 9/15/2019.

[2] Victoria Speaks-Fold, Ed.D, *Early Childhood News; The Professional Resource for Teachers and Parents; Accommodating Different Personalities and Temperaments,* http://www.psychpage.com/family/library/temperm.htm. Accessed 9/15/2019.

[3] Sick Kids Staff, *About Kid's Health; Trusted answers from The Hospital for Sick Children; Sick Kids; Temperament,* https://www.aboutkidshealth.ca/Article?contentid=499&language=English. Accessed 9/15/2019.

[4] Diane Weiss, M.S., *Parenting Works LLC; Handout; Nine Temperament Traits and Three Temperament Types,* http://www.pa-pat.org/wp-content/uploads/sites/9/2016/06/HANDOUT-Nine-Temperament-Traits-Three-Temperament-Types.pdf. Accessed 9/15/2019.

40% of children have an easy temperament. Usually, these babies are easily toilet trained, learn to sleep through the night, have regular feeding and nap routines, approach new situations and people pleasantly and adapt to change quickly. They are generally cheerful and express distress or frustration mildly. Parents of children that are identified as being easy often feel good about their parenting skills and how they are doing as parents.

Children with a difficult temperament tend to have intense reactions, irregular daily routines, an overall negative mood as well as long and frequent crying episodes. These children often withdraw from or are slow to adapt to new experiences. The difficult category includes about 10% of babies and children.

The child with this temperament may be hard to get to sleep through the night, feeding and nap schedules may change from day to day and toilet training may be challenging because of irregular bowel movements. This type of child often expresses an unpleasant or disagreeable mood. They tend to adapt slowly, are fussy or may even cry loudly at anything new. Parents of difficult babies sometimes question their parenting skills and feel like they are doing something wrong.

The term difficult was established in original research on temperament. However, it has a somewhat negative connotation. Words such as spirited or feisty have been suggested as alternatives. It is important to note that valuable behavioral traits like assertiveness, persistence and decisiveness are also common characteristics of children with difficult temperament types.

Children with a slow-to-warm-up temperament typically have a low activity level, are somewhat negative and display a low intensity of mood. They tend to withdraw from or are slow to adapt to new things. These children are often thought of as shy or sensitive and maybe even fearful. Between 5% and 15% of babies and children are identified as being slow-to-warm-up.

These children do not like to be pushed into things. They typically stand at the edge of a group and cling quietly to a parent when taken to a store, birthday party or childcare for the first time. If the child is pressured to join the group, the child's shyness immediately becomes worse. When allowed to gradually become accustomed to new surroundings, this child can acclimate and become an active, happy member of the group. Parents that expect a child to quickly adapt to or engage in new situations can become frustrated when their slow-to-warm-up child is clingy or withdrawn instead.

Each of the three major temperaments has strengths and challenges. Flexible, easy children are adaptable, react mildly to change and have consistent patterns of eating and sleeping. Children with feisty, spirited, difficult temperaments have intense reactions to change and irregular patterns of eating and sleeping. Children that are cautious and slow to warm up tend to withdraw from new experiences and do not adapt to change easily.

No one temperament is superior to another. The behaviors associated with each are on a continuum ranging from mild to severe. Only about 65% of all children and babies fit into one of the main categories of temperament. Rather than having the characteristics of just one category, the remaining children have a combination of the qualities found in the three main temperament types.

Goodness of Fit

Goodness of fit is a term originally used by Thomas and Chess in their research about temperament.[1] It describes how well the expectations of a baby's environment fit together with the baby's temperament.[2] Typically, parents and caregivers are the most important people in a baby's life and the most influential

---

[1] Hipson, Will & Séguin, Daniel. (2017). *Goodness of Fit Model,* https://www.researchgate.net/publication/313123770_Goodness_of_Fit_M odel. Accessed 9/15/2019.

[2] The Center for Parenting Education, *Understanding Goodness of Fit,* https://centerforparentingeducation.org/library-of-articles/child-development/understanding-goodness-of-fit. Accessed 9/15/2019.

factors in a baby's daily environment. Caregivers have preferences and expectations about their children's behavior. Parents may or may not be aware of those expectations. The expectations may be unspoken but nonetheless strong and powerful. Since primary caregivers play such an important role in the lives of babies, the congruence between their expectations and the child's temperament is foundational to establishing a good fit. In other words, goodness of fit is not just about the individual parent or the child but about how their temperaments fit together.

An example of goodness of fit is a relaxed parent that appreciates and admires the intensity and focus that is displayed in a difficult child. On the other hand, a different parent that is easy-going or has a low energy level may have difficulty dealing with a child who is very active and intense. This is an example of a poor fit between parent and child. Although they may experience some challenges, with understanding and intentional effort the relationship can be strengthened and increasingly supportive.

Another example that is often seen with a feisty child is the child's tendency to have an intense, noisy reaction to a situation. When frustrated, the child may quickly escalate and have a temper tantrum. If the caregiver scolds, placates or tries to force the child to change, it usually only reinforces the difficult behavior. Often the best way to deal with such outbursts is just to wait for the child to calm down. Caregivers who do not understand that this behavior is characteristic of the difficult temperament type may feel resentment toward the child for being so difficult to manage. Understanding, patience and consistency, on the other hand, will probably lead to a better fit and most likely result in a more positive adjustment to the future demands of life. Nurturing a child with a difficult temperament can be challenging. In order to maintain perspective, parents can benefit from scheduled time away from their child for much needed rest and respite.

The challenge with slow-to-warm-up children is helping them overcome their fear of new people and situations. A child with this temperament needs a positive environment where new stimuli are presented gradually and repeatedly. Instead of being forced, the baby needs to be encouraged. When pressured to hurry, the child with this temperament tends to become increasingly negative. The need to support a child over and over with the demands of socialization can test the caregiver's patience and can eventually result in frustration and anger. Persistence, gentleness and flexibility are keys to successfully parenting a child that is slow to adapt.

Each child is wired with a unique temperament that is part of who they are for a lifetime. The child does not choose its own temperament. Parents do not choose their child's temperament. Parents, however, do have the opportunity to build the best fit they can between their own expectations and the behavioral style of their child.[1]

A good fit between parent and child can sometimes be challenging to achieve. Every parent has a temperament style and that style can influence the expectations parents have for their baby. Often the experiences parents had as children with the demands and expectations of their own caregivers can impact the expectations they have for their child's behavioral pattern. For example, a parent that was raised by an anxious or depressed caregiver may feel challenged, anxious or frustrated by a slow-to-warm up baby that reacts timidly to new people and environments. The baby's reactions may serve as an uncomfortable or even painful reminder of the parents' own childhood.[2]

---

[1] Healthy Place.com Staff Writer, *Healthy Place for Your Mental Health; Goodness of Fit: How Temperament Determines Need,*
https://www.healthyplace.com/parenting/challenge-of-difficult-children/goodness-of-fit-how-temperament-determines-need. Accessed 9/15/2019.
[2] Sick Kids Staff, *About Kid's Health; Trusted answers from The Hospital for Sick Children, Sick Kids;* Temperament,
https://www.aboutkidshealth.ca/Article?contentid=499&language=English. Accessed 9/15/2019.

Parents often benefit from reflecting on their own temperaments and thinking about how their expectations would affect their child's reactions. This can be particularly important when there is a mismatch between a parent's emotional and behavioral reactions and a child's temperament. If expectations do not match a child's temperament, a parent's reactions can exaggerate a child's behavioral and emotional issues which can lead to a deterioration in the interactions and relationship between parent and child.

Goodness of fit can extend beyond the parental relationship with the baby.[1] If a baby has additional caregivers or attends childcare outside the home, it may be important to consider how well the environment accommodates the baby's emotional and behavioral characteristics. Later, when a child attends school, the fit between the child and the classroom environment and the teacher's temperament can be significant factors. When thinking about temperament, it is important to remember a child's negative traits can be subdued, and positive traits can be enhanced if the environmental expectations are adapted to accommodate the child's temperament.

Learning Modalities

Learning modalities are the preferential pathways individuals use to understand and retain information. Also known as learning styles, learning modalities refer to the consistent way the senses are used to respond to stimuli during the learning process.[2] Children learn in different ways. In education, a number of different modalities have been identified including three that are

---

[1] Natasha Boskic, *Early Childhood Intervention: Module One–Typical and Atypical Development; Parenting Styles and the Goodness of Fit Model,* http://blogs.ubc.ca/earlychildhoodintervention1/2010/12/03/parenting-styles-and-the-goddess-of-fit-model. Accessed 9/15/2019.

[2] Madison Michell, Edmentum Blog, *Kinesthetic, Visual, Auditory, Tactile, Oh My! What Are Learning Modalities and How Can You Incorporate Them in the Classroom?* Monday, September 25, 2017. http://blog.edmentum.com/kinesthetic-visual-auditory-tactile-oh-my-what-are-learning-modalities-and-how-can-you-incorporate. Accessed 9/15/2019.

considered the basic learning styles. They are visual, auditory, and kinesthetic/tactile.[1,2]

Visual learners absorb information by seeing and watching. For them, the most effective instruction needs to provide opportunities to visualize and illustrate knowledge, skills and concepts. They prefer to learn using visual representations such as graphs, posters, maps and displays. It is worth noting that these learners may not comprehend or understand when they are told how to do something; they need to see it.

Auditory learners acquire knowledge by listening and talking about what they are hearing. They usually need to have things explained orally, sometimes find written instructions to be challenging and like to discuss information in groups rather than work alone. Learning preferences for this group include repetition, summaries, discussions, lectures, and stories. Sometimes auditory learners look like they are not paying attention, because their listening skills are more developed than their visual skills.

Kinesthetic/tactile learners gain knowledge by doing and touching. They are active learners that are motivated when given an opportunity to actually do whatever is being learned. They like to move around while listening or talking and want to touch things in order to learn about them. Active learners prefer to learn through hands-on activities, field trips, physical activity and manipulating objects.

Kinesthetic learners often have difficulty sitting still. They tend to move constantly and usually need frequent breaks when learning. Because of their high activity level, kinesthetic learners can be misdiagnosed as having attention deficit or

---

[1] Donald Clark, A Big Dog & Little Dog's Performance Juxtaposition; Visual, Auditory, and Kinesthetic Learning Styles (VAK), http://www.nwlink.com/~donclark/hrd/styles/vakt.html. Accessed 9/15/2019.

[2] Fiona Baker; *Learning Styles in Children*, July 03, 2017, https://www.kidspot.com.au/school/primary/learning-and-behaviour/learning-styles-in-children/news-story/2c188e7d8ca8d273b2f441fcae6ae1ba. Accessed 9/15/2019.

behavioral issues. More traditional instruction that depends on visual or auditory learning styles can be challenging for them.[1]

Most learners use all three main modalities, and possibly others as well, to learn new information and process new experiences. However, it is thought that most individuals have a dominant learning style. In other words, individuals may have preferred styles of instruction that makes learning more engaging and meaningful for them. Although not definitively established in research, some educational environments support intentionally using a child's preferred style of learning expecting that it will result in the most effective learning. Probably the more commonly accepted practice is to use a variety of modalities with the idea that it will be optimal for maximizing learning. It is notable that some learners prefer one style of learning for one thing but prefer another style or a combination of styles for learning something else.

Parents can help their children learn more effectively when they know each child's preferred learning modality. A child's preferred learning style can usually be identified by intentionally observing and listening to the child during daily routines and activities like play.

It is also important for parents to recognize their own favored learning styles as well as the preferred styles of any other caregivers that frequently interact with the child. Adults tend to communicate and teach using their own favorite style. By being aware of their own dominant learning method as well as the child's preferred style, parents can adapt the guidance they provide for instruction, teachable moments and new experiences with the child.

Adults can also support the child by offering opportunities to adapt to other learning styles. Less dominant styles can be developed, and the more dominant style can mature and develop even further. This may be especially

[1] Tracy Harrington-Atkinson, *Barbe's VAK Learning Style*, September 7, 2017, http://tracyharringtonatkinson.com/barbes-vak-learning-style. Accessed 9/15/2019.

important for very active children as parents help prepare them for the transition to the structured environment of formal education.[1]

Parenting Styles

Parenting style refers to the overall approach or a combination of strategies used by parents to raise their children. Perhaps the most commonly referenced styles of parenting in the United States were identified by developmental psychologist Diane Baumrind in the 1960s. She recognized four basic types of parenting styles: authoritarian, permissive, uninvolved and authoritative. Each type implements a different approach to raising children and can be identified by a number of distinct characteristics.[2]

Authoritarian parents are often thought of as disciplinarians. Punishment is common with a strict discipline style. Communication typically flows one-way from parent to child. Rules are usually non-negotiable and not explained. Parents with this style have high expectations with limited flexibility and are typically less nurturing.

Permissive or indulgent parents mostly let their children do what they want. They tend to offer limited guidance and are more like friends than parents. They establish few, if any rules, and generally let children figure out solutions to problems on their own. Parents in this category tend to be warm and nurturing. Communication is open with parents having few expectations and offering little direction.

Uninvolved parents devote little time or energy to meeting children's basic needs and seem to expect children to raise themselves. They have no particular discipline style. This group of parents offers little nurturing. Communication is

---

[1] Time for Learning, *Learning Styles*, https://www.time4learning.com/learning-styles.shtml. Accessed 9/15/2019.
[2] Bright Horizons®; *What Is My Parenting Style? Four Types of Parenting*, https://www.brighthorizons.com/family-resources/e-family-news/parenting-style-four-types-of-parenting. Accessed 9/15/2019.

limited. There are few or no expectations of children.

Uninvolved parents may be neglectful because they are focused on their own personal problems. For example, a parent with mental health or substance abuse issues may not be capable of consistently caring for a child's physical or emotional needs. Some uninvolved parents are overwhelmed with concerns, like work, paying bills, and managing a households. Still others may lack knowledge and understanding.

Authoritative parents are nurturing with high expectations. Rules of discipline are clearly stated and reasons are explained. Communication is frequent and appropriate to the child's level of understanding. This parenting style is sometimes simplified by describing it as being firm but kind.

Parents that utilize the authoritative style often expect a lot of their children, but the children may have input into goals. Children with parents who demonstrate this style tend to be self-disciplined and think for themselves. This style is thought to be most beneficial for children.

As reported in *Parenting for Brain, Healthy Brain, Happy Kids*, each of the four parenting styles is correlated to the following characteristics and effects in their children.[1]

Children of authoritarian parents
- Tend to have an unhappy disposition.
- Are less independent.
- Appear insecure.
- Possess lower self-esteem.
- Exhibit more behavioral problems.
- Perform worse academically.
- Have poorer social skills.
- Are more prone to mental issues.

---

[1] Parenting For Brain, Healthy Brain, Happy Kids. *4 Parenting Styles – Characteristics and Effects*, Updated 07/18/2019, https://www.parentingforbrain.com/4-baumrind-parenting-styles. Accessed 9/15/2019.

Children of permissive parenting
- Cannot follow rules.
- Have worse self-control.
- Possess egocentric tendencies.
- Encounter more problems in relationships and social interactions.

Children of uninvolved parent:
- Are more impulsive.
- Cannot self-regulate emotion.
- Encounter more delinquency and addictions problems.
- Have more mental issues, e.g. suicidal behavior in adolescents.

Children of authoritative parents:
- Appear happy and content.
- Are more independent.
- Achieve higher academic success.
- Develop good self-esteem.
- Interact with peers using competent social skills.
- Have better mental health; less depression, anxiety, suicide attempts, delinquency, alcohol and drug use.
- Exhibit less violent tendencies.

Each of the parenting styles can be summarized in a few words. The focus of the authoritarian style is on obedience and punishment rather than discipline. The theme of the permissive style is "kids will be kids" so there is no need to enforce rules. The uninvolved parenting style provides children with little guidance, nurturing or attention. Finally, the authoritative style enforces rules while maintaining a positive relationship.[1]

---

[1] Amy Morin, LCSW, reviewed by Steven Gans, MD, *Very Well Family; 4 Types of Parenting Styles and Their Effects on Kids; What's Your Parenting Style?*, updated September 19, 2018, https://www.verywellfamily.com/types-of-

The authoritative style is considered to be most beneficial for children, because after decades of studies, researchers consistently found that authoritative parenting is linked to the best outcomes for children. Ideally, the authoritative parenting style supports healthy growth and development by maintaining a positive parent-child relationship while establishing respectful authority.

Some new parents may have unpleasant memories of their own childhoods and, in light of past negative experiences, vow they will raise their children differently. Parents may want to make changes, but with the pressures of life they can easily just drift into old family patterns of behavior. Meaningful change cannot really happen without effort. After learning new concepts and behaviors, parents can make informed decisions about the child-rearing practices they choose to implement with their own children.

parenting-styles-1095045. Accessed 9/15/2019.

CHAPTER 3

Tools for Nurturing Language, Literacy and Prophecy

Emerging Language

Language development actually begins before birth. Towards the end of pregnancy, an unborn child can hear sounds and speech from outside the mother's body. At birth, crying is a baby's primary means of communication. Almost immediately, language begins to develop by means of repetition and imitation as the baby has opportunities to interact with parents, family and other caregivers. Relationship is a vital component in language development. That is a key concept. Language can only be learned in the context of relationship![1]

Here's how it works. When a caregiver speaks to an infant, the infant responds. Then the caregiver responds back to the infant. If still engaged, the baby responds again. This responsive cycle is repeated over and over. The ongoing back and forth interaction that is necessary for language development is called reciprocity. It is also known as serve and return. In the

---

[1] Froma P. Roth, PhD, CCC-SLP, Diane R. Paul, PhD, CCC-SLP, Ann-Mari Pierotti, MA, CCC-SLP, *Let's Talk, For People with Special Communication Needs, Emergent Literacy: Early Reading and Writing Development*; American Speech-Language-Hearing Association (ASHA), 2006.
http://www.healthofchildren.com/L/Language-Development.html. Accessed 9/15/2019.

language cycle, caregivers follow the child's lead. Little ones can tire quickly but, over time, their ability to be attentive usually increases. Through observation, caregivers learn to read children's cues and understand if they are disengaged or still engaged and ready to continue the cycle. As caregivers observe, listen and respond, interactions build a stronger bond with the child and develop a parent-child relationship that is the foundational building block for vigorous language development.

The process of developing communication skills can be referred to as emerging language. Young children first develop receptive language. Receptive language is the ability for young ones to understand what they hear. They begin to recognize and attach meaning to accompanying gestures. In this way, they learn to receive communications. Next, expressive language or the ability to express thoughts is developed. This involves trying to talk and experimenting with various ways of expressing through speaking and gesturing.

Babies all around the world make identical sounds and babblings in this early stage of language development. This includes those who are deaf. Infants are born with the capacity to learn any language. The language they learn becomes determined by social interaction. Relationship is an essential component of emerging language development.

In a well-known study conducted by the late University of Kansas child psychologists Betty Hart and Todd R. Risley, 42 infants that were just learning to talk were observed over time. The researchers tracked how parents and children interacted as well as the children's total word exposure. The families involved in the research included 13 middle-class households, 10 each professional and working-class household, and six living on public assistance.[1]

The researchers found that children from professional

---

[1] Leaders Project (Hart & Risley, 1995), *Meaningful Differences in the Everyday Experience of Young American Children*, March 17, 2013. https://www.leadersproject.org/2013/03/17/meaningful-differences-in-the-everyday-experience-of-young-american-children. Accessed 9/15/2019.

families averaged hearing more than 2,150 words an hour. Those in working-class families heard about 1,250 words. Children in families receiving assistance heard little more than 600 words an hour. Along with the significant word gap, researchers later found differences in the quality of interactions. The children of professionals heard more unique words and were more than twice as likely to have experienced encouraging conversational patterns rather than discouraging conversational patterns. Study results suggested that a talkative parenting style impacted the correlation between socioeconomic status and children's later linguistic and academic development.[1]

The results of this study can be applied to all parents of infants, toddlers and preschoolers. Like a sportscaster announces a ballgame, caregivers are encouraged to talk with and listen to the children in their care. Describe activities throughout the day and explain everything that is happening. For example, give baby a play-by-play account of changing diapers, getting dressed and feeding. Ask questions. Tell stories. Read books. Sing songs. Repeat rhymes. As the child develops language skills, engage in conversations that give both parent and child opportunities to listen and speak. This type of relational interaction is essential for enhancing all kinds of emerging skills

Language development can typically be divided into three main categories. The first group is the pre-linguistic stage which is the time before most speech and language has developed. It usually lasts from birth to about 18 months. The next stage is the time when speech and language are just beginning that is known as the early emerging language stage. It typically lasts from about a year and a half to age two. Sometime around the second year, the developing language stage begins. During this time, language development continues, and many

---

[1] Sarah D. Sparks, *Key to Vocabulary Gap Is Quality of Conversation, Not Dearth of Words*, Kansas University; Life Span Institute, April 21, 2015, https://lsi.ku.edu/news/key-to-vocabulary-gap-is-quality-of-conversation-not-dearth-of-words. Accessed 9/15/2019.

language milestones are achieved. These stages are quite fluid and differ greatly from child to child. Typically, children progress through developmental milestones in the same sequence or order, but the time frames often vary considerably from one child to another.[1]

Because early communication skills develop very quickly, caregivers need to be attentive to changes in a child's abilities. Speech and language developmental growth charts can help track a child's progress and make sure every milestone is met. Milestone checklists that include all developmental domains can be accessed at the Centers for Disease Control and Prevention (CDC) website. The printable checklists are available for ages 2, 4, 6, 9, 12 and 18 months and then annually for ages 2, 3, 4 and 5 years.[2]

Infants are able to tune in to the human voice and show a special preference for higher pitch of female voices. Using a special form of baby talk with high-pitched speech that is exaggerated and repetitive can be purposeful and effective. This type of baby talk, also known as parentese, is especially interesting to little ones and often captures their attention.[3]

Supporting early language development should begin with reinforcing what the baby is already doing. When caregivers support a baby's early attempts at communication, language development can progress more quickly. Talking and

---

[1] Robin Zeller, Ph.D., *Sound Hearing Audiology and Speech; Language Development Overview; Stages of Language Development,*
http://audiologyspeechphd.com/sound-hearing-audiology-and-speech/language-development-overview. Accessed 9/15/2019.
[2] Center for Disease Control and Prevention (CDC), *Developmental Milestones, Milestone printable checklists that include all developmental domains are available for ages 2, 4, 6, 9, 12 and 18 months and then annually for ages 2, 3, 4 and 5 years,*
https://www.cdc.gov/ncbddd/actearly/milestones/index.html. Accessed 9/15/2019.
[3] The Center for Early Literacy Learning (CELL), funded by the U.S. Department of Education, Office of Special Education Programs (H326B060010), *Talk to Me in Parentese,* 2010,
http://www.earlyliteracylearning.org/cellpract_parent/infants/PG_1_I_Talk 2Me.pdf. Accessed 9/15/2019.

communicating usually flow naturally during parent-child interactions.

Developing language and communication skills is often linked with play. Both should be fun! While observing and interacting with a child during play as well as other activities, parents gain understanding of the child's skill level. The goal for parents is to help the baby reach forward to the next level of skill development. For example, if the child says one word, the goal would be to repeat that word and then expand the communication by adding two or three more words or even a short sentence. If the child says, "truck," the caregiver could expand the communication by saying "big truck" or "that's a fast truck."[1]

It is important to follow the child's lead and check frequently to be sure the baby is still engaged. Little ones tire quickly. When children are rested and their needs have been met, they are more likely to be empowered to try out new words and communicate in new ways. Parents also need to be attentive to nonverbal communication; it can be foundational in the development of verbal skills. As caregivers observe, listen to baby's communications and become aware of baby's interests, they become increasingly equipped to help successfully guide the child toward the next level of language development.

Cycle of Learning Language

Listen! Observe! Adapt and expand!

- Listen to the baby's verbalizations.
- Observe the baby's behaviors.
- Adapt to the baby's behavior. Follow the baby's lead. Expand on the baby's verbalizations.

---

[1] Rachel Cortese, MS, CCC-SLP, *Child Mind Institute; Helping Toddlers Expand Language Skills; Tips for encouraging kids age 0-5 to talk*, https://childmind.org/article/helping-toddlers-expand-their-language-skills. Accessed 9/15/2019.

- If the child is still engaged, continue language interactions with the baby.
- If the child has disengaged, take a break and try again later when the baby is ready.

Emerging Literacy

Emerging literacy, emergent literacy and early literacy are all terms that express the idea that learning literacy skills begins long before children go to school to start formal education. Early literacy does not mean early reading. But it does mean that many of the skills that are necessary for both reading and writing can be developed when children are very young. Along with early speech and language development, a child's knowledge of reading and writing can begin shortly after birth and continue through the preschool years.

Beginning at birth, or even before, what parents do every day helps prepare their children to become successful readers. A print rich environment offers a variety of opportunities to interact with many different forms of print. Literacy skills are developed through interactions that include activities like talking, singing, reading, writing and playing. Relationship with nurturing caregivers is foundational to literacy development.

The emphasis of early literacy learning focuses on the natural unfolding of skills through positive interactions between young children, caring adults and, in some cases, older children. Providing a print-rich environment that encourages exploring, enjoying and playing with books is ideal for developing early literacy skills. Providing appropriate materials and frequent opportunities for activities like singing, repeating finger plays and rhymes, listening to stories, identifying words, recognizing symbols, and scribbling are the building blocks of both language and literacy development.

The concept of early literacy can be summarized with

the following key statements.[1] Throughout the early years of a child's life, early literacy is an ongoing developmental process. The development of language, reading and writing skills are all connected and happen simultaneously. Relationship is the basic foundation for literacy skill development and early literacy skills are built through positive interactions with caring people and age-appropriate literacy materials.

In emergent literacy, children learn through observing others with books and participating in informal literacy activities using materials like books, paper, crayons and markers. In this natural, informal and pleasant way, children gain important literacy prerequisites. Early knowledge about literacy provides an important foundation for children to build on later during more formal teaching of literacy skills. Preschoolers with knowledge in these areas generally develop into better readers and writers than preschoolers without these experiences. Providing very young children with literacy-rich learning opportunities and environments is key to the development of emergent literacy skills during preschool years.[2]

Children's Literature
Books, books, books! Giving young children opportunities to interact with books is one of the most effective ways to develop the skills needed for later success in learning to read and write. Providing children with a print-rich environment that offers a variety of ways to interact with different forms of print is optimal for language and literacy development.

The goal of early literacy is not that babies and toddlers learn to read and write through formal instruction. Instead, the

[1] Zero to Three Parenting Resource, *Early Literacy Handout, What We Know About Early Literacy and Language Development*, February 25, 2003. https://www.zerotothree.org/resources/300-what-we-know-about-early-literacy-and-language-development. Accessed 9/15/19.
[2] Laura M. Justice, Joan Kaderavek, *Using Shared Storybook Reading to Promote Emergent Literacy,* First Published March 1, 2002 Research Article. https://journals.sagepub.com/doi/abs/10.1177/00400599020340 0401?journalCode=tcxa. Accessed 9/15/2019.

focus is on encouraging the natural unfolding of the emerging literary process with an emphasis on positive interactions with books and caring adults. Literacy materials and experiences need to be appropriate for the developmental level of each child. The National Association for the Education of Young Children (NAEYC) explains developmentally appropriate practice using these core concepts.[1]

- **Knowing about child development and learning.**
  Understanding typical development and learning at different ages is a crucial starting point. This knowledge, based on research, helps us predict which experiences will support children's learning and development.
- **Knowing what is individually appropriate.**
  What we learn about specific children helps us refine decisions about how to teach and care for each child as an individual. By continually observing children's play and interaction with the physical environment and others, we learn about each child's interests, abilities, and developmental progress.
- **Knowing what is culturally important.**
  We must make an effort to get to know the children's families and learn about the values, expectations, and factors that shape their lives at home and in their communities. This background information helps us provide

---

[1] National Association for the Education of Young Children (NAEYC); *Developmentally Appropriate Practice (DAP) Introduction.* https://www.naeyc.org/resources/topics/dap. Accessed 9/15/2019.

meaningful, relevant, and respectful learning experiences for each child and family.

Caregivers can support literacy development by providing experiences that are appropriate for the age, individuality and cultural environment of each child. The cultural environment can include the child's immediate family, extended family, neighborhood, community, race, ethnicity, region, and nation. It is particularly important to recognize that each family is unique and usually cultivates their own culture.

As children grow and develop, their skill levels progress and their interests change. Babies and infants enjoy having books read to them and also respond to singing and music. During tummy time on the floor, infants like to look at board books with simple pictures that are propped-up nearby. Toddlers enjoy mouthing and exploring washable board books that have brightly colored pictures of familiar things like other babies or animals and have simple rhymes or only a few words. Twos and threes enjoy books that tell simple stories, rhyming books, bedtime books and books about colors, shapes and numbers. Fours and fives enjoy books that are longer with more details, books that are rhyming, rhythmical and repetitive and books with stories about life experiences like going to school or welcoming a new sibling.[1]

Children's literature can help foster skill development in emerging language and literacy. Ideas for interacting with children and books include the following:

- Let the child choose the book.
- Let the child hold the book and turn the pages.
- It's okay not to finish the book.
- It's okay to "read" the book at the child's pace.

---

[1] Lauren Lowry Hanen, Certified SLP and Clinical Staff Writer, The Hanen Centre, the Hanen Way, *Sharing Books with Preschoolers*, http://www.hanen.org/Helpful-Info/Fun-Activities/Sharing-books-with-Preschoolers,-the-Hanen-Way.aspx. Accessed 9/15/2019.

- It's okay to simplify the story or just talk about the pictures and not read the words.
- It's okay to look at the same book over and over again.
- It's okay to pause, wait quietly and give the child an opportunity for self-expression.
- Try acting out a familiar story or a scene from story.
- Frequently take time to repeat rhymes and finger plays.
- Write down preschooler's stories including captions for their illustrations.

Every day parents need to spend some time exploring books with their child. When reading out loud, point to or track the text with a finger. Show the cover page pointing out the book title and author. Be expressive and make the story come alive. Watch for opportunities to be dramatic and use different voices. Talk or sing about the pictures. With preschoolers, let the child read or tell the story. Ask questions and encourage the child to ask questions, too. Make sharing books and enjoying parent-child interactions part of every day!

Emerging Prophecy

Prophets speak. The very definition of a prophet includes the concept of speaking. Specifically, it is speaking the heart and mind of God. Prophets are also often asked to read and write as directed by Divine inspiration. Examples include Moses writing the Book of the Law in Deuteronomy 31:24, Ezra reading the Law to the people in Nehemiah 8, and Daniel reading the writing on the wall in Daniel 5. An instance of both prophetic reading and writing is found in Habakkuk.

> The LORD answered me and said:
> "Write the vision
> And make it plain on tablets,
> That he may run who reads it."
>
> Habakkuk 2:2

Of course, just like everyone else, prophets are born without the ability to speak. In order to effectively use their God-given spiritual gifts, prophets should learn spoken and written language as well as other literacy skills. For all children, that learning is an ongoing process. It should begin very early and be developed step-by-step over time.

The skills that are essential for learning language, reading and writing are many of the same skills needed for developing prophecy and other spiritual gifts. That means emerging language, literacy and prophecy often develop simultaneously and are intertwined. Since all these skills are best developed in the context of relationships and nurturing interactions, parents and caregivers have an enormous opportunity to activate and cultivate their children's potential. As parents become increasingly aware of their children's development, they can be purposeful in preparing an environment that is optimal for that development.

Think about a butterfly that is preparing to leave its cocoon. Consider a rosebud opening from a small bud to a beautiful blossom. Reflect on a chick breaking out of its shell. All these processes demonstrate the concept of emerging. None of them can be controlled, hurried or forced. The most effective way to facilitate emergence of any kind is to provide a safe, stable and nurturing environment and allow the process to unfold at its own pace. The beginning skills needed for language, literacy and prophecy can grow and thrive when they are intentionally cultivated and nurtured in the context of relationship. It's important to remember that parents and caregivers can identify and steward their children's gifts, but both the children and the gifts are given by God. He is sovereign. He can give gifts to anyone, anywhere, at any time. In France, in the area of the Ct'vennes, an amazing prophetic movement is recorded between 1688 and 1702. In the midst of severe persecution, there are powerful testimonies of teenagers, young children and even babies in their cribs that prophesied and ministered with Holy Spirit. These illiterate children were supernaturally gifted in giving messages in French even though they did not know the French language. Father God, in the

Name of Jesus, by the power of Holy Spirit is the Giver of all gifts. He is the Source of all.[1]

Luke 1:40-45 is an example of prophetic expression when a child is in the womb, unborn. When Mary was pregnant with Jesus, she went to visit her cousin Elizabeth who was pregnant with John the Baptist.

Notice how John, who was not born, responded to the Presence of the unborn Jesus.

When Mary arrived, entered the house and greeted Elizabeth, "the baby within Elizabeth's womb jumped and kicked. Suddenly, Elizabeth was filled to overflowing with Holy Spirit! With a loud voice she prophesied with power.

> Mary! You are a woman given the highest favor and privilege above all others.
> For your child is destined to bring God great delight.
> How did I deserve such a remarkable honor to have the mother of my Lord come and visit me?
> The moment you came in the door and greeted me, my baby danced inside me with ecstatic joy! Great favor is upon you, for you have believed every word spoken to you from the Lord."
>
> Luke 1:40-45, TPT

Mary and Elizabeth established a prophetic environment that activated the prophetic in their unborn babies. The prenatal environment has a powerful impact in both the natural and spiritual realms. Prophetic gifts are God-given and present before birth.

---

[1] Walters, Kathie, *The Child Prophets of France 1688-1702, Posted June 5, 2011,* http://injesus.com/message-archives/prophetic/kathiewaltersministy/the-child-prophets-of-france-16881702. Accessed 9/15/2019.

Prophets and Learning Modalities

Think about God's call to young Jeremiah. Review what God did to train Jeremiah and develop his prophetic skills. Consider the most dominant learning styles; visual, auditory and tactile/kinesthetic.

> The word of the LORD came to me: "What do
> you **see**, Jeremiah?"
> "I **see** the branch of an almond tree," I replied.
> The LORD said to me, "You have **seen** correctly,
> for I am **watching** to **see** that my word is
> fulfilled."
> The word of the LORD came to me again: "What
> do you see?"
> "I see a pot that is boiling," I answered. "It is
> tilting toward us from the north."
> Jeremiah 1: 11-13, NIV, emphasis mine

Notice the words in the passage that reference vision. Notice the question, *"What do you see?"* The same question is asked again. Notice that each time it is asked, Jeremiah's quick answer means he must have been equipped to easily see what God saw. It seems likely Jeremiah's preferred learning style was visual.

Amos and Zechariah are also prophets that might have preferred the visual learning style. Amos 7:8 and 8:2 as well as Zechariah 4:2 and 5:2 refer to what is seen. Habakkuk is another prophet that makes visual references like the one in Habakkuk 2:2.

> Then the LORD answered me and said:
> "Write the vision
> And make it plain on tablets,
> That he may run who reads it.
> Jeremiah 24:3, emphasis mine

When God first called Jeremiah to be a prophet, he was young, but Samuel may have been even younger when God called him. Hannah, Samuel's mother, was childless and cried out to God asking for a son. In return, she promised to dedicate her son to God. True to her word, Hannah brought Samuel to the house of the Lord shortly after he was weaned to be raised by the elderly prophet Eli.

One night while Samuel was sleeping, he heard someone call his name. Thinking it was Eli, Samuel ran to him. But Eli had not called. Samuel went back to bed. The same sequence happened three times. Finally, Eli realized that God was calling Samuel. Eli gave Samuel these instructions.

> Eli said to Samuel, "Go, lie down; and it shall be, if He calls you, that you must say, 'Speak, LORD, for Your servant hears.'" So, Samuel went and lay down in his place.
>
> Now the LORD came and stood and called as at other times, "Samuel! Samuel!"
>
> And Samuel answered, "Speak, for Your servant hears."
>
> Then the LORD said to Samuel: "Behold, I will do something in Israel at which both ears of everyone who hears it will tingle."
>
> 1 Samuel 3:9-11, NIV

In this passage, notice the words that refer to hearing and ears. The primary learning style God used to communicate with Samuel appears to be auditory. In the New Testament, there are other important references to hearing. Paul wrote, "Faith comes by hearing, and hearing by the word of God" (Romans 10:17). John writes, "He who has an ear, let him hear what the Spirit says to the churches. To him who overcomes I will give to eat from the tree of life, which is in the midst of the Paradise of God" (Revelation 2:7). There are more than 40 references to hearing in the Book of Revelation.

King David was identified as a prophet in Acts 2:29-30. An example of a prophetic word given by David is found in Psalm 22:1, "My God, My God, why have You forsaken Me?" Those are the same unforgettable words Jesus spoke about a thousand years later when He was dying on the cross.

As a shepherd, David protected the sheep, even to the point of killing a bear and lion when they threatened (1 Samuel 17:34, 36). When everyone else was intimidated and afraid, he won a victory for Israel by killing the giant Goliath using a rock and a sling shot (1 Samuel 17:50). Later, David was appointed commander of the army and was well-known for defeating tens of thousands (1 Samuel 18:7).

David was musical (1 Samuel 18:10). He was known for his exuberant, undignified worship with shouting and dancing (2 Samuel 6:5, 14, 22). David, as a psalmist, wrote many of the most beloved and poetic psalms including Psalm 16, 23, 42, 51, 103, 139 and 145. David was a man of powerful action that expressed intense feeling. It seems likely that David preferred a kinesthetic/tactile learning style. That seemed to be his leadership style, too.

Three different prophets that, according to biblical accounts, illustrated three different styles of learning. Jeremiah prophesied using the visual learning style. Samuel's auditory gift was activated when he heard God speak prophetic words. David demonstrated kinesthetic/tactile gifts in wide range of diverse activities and situations throughout his lifetime.

Children's Literature and Prophecy

Books and more books! Giving young children opportunities to interact with books is one of the most effective ways to develop the skills needed for later success in learning to read and write. Children's literature also helps with the identification and development of spiritual gifts. As previously stated, parents and caregivers do not choose their children's God-given gifts. They can, however, choose and prepare an environment for their children that is rich with opportunities for learning. Such an environment includes choosing books for children with intentionality and purpose. For example, parents can pick books that contain prophetic learning styles, thus, providing very young children with opportunities for developing language, literacy and prophetic skills.

Jeremiah and the Visual Learning Style

When God first visited Jeremiah, He asked, *What do you see?* The children's book *Brown Bear, Brown Bear*[1] repeats that same question. The book uses rhyme, rhythm and repetition to teach the names of colors and animals. Reading it is a pre-literacy activity that parents and children can enjoy together. Along with all that, consider the possibility that *Brown Bear, Brown Bear* can facilitate development of prophetic skills, particularly when combined with additional activities.

Spontaneous games are usually great fun for children. A simple game that flows naturally after becoming familiar with this book involves asking *What do you see?* and then listening to and observing the child's response. Just say the child's name twice followed by *What do you see?*

This type of game can include other caregivers and siblings. It can be played anywhere; indoors, outdoors, in the car, backyard, or park. It can be changed and adapted to fit the child and situation. The important thing is to remember to be creative and have fun!

A made-up game like the one described above offers children an opportunity to use language and verbal skills. It can assist with the development of vocabulary expansion, creativity, awareness of the environment, observation, taking turns and finding out what the child is thinking about and seeing. It may also give insight into the child's learning style and other preferences.

Blake Healy is an example of someone that had a dominant visual learning style from a very young age. The reader is strongly encouraged to read Mr. Healy's book, *The Veil*.[2] Although the extent, intensity and power of his gift is rare,

---

[1] Bill Martin, Jr., *Brown Bear, Brown Bear, What Do You See?* (New York, NY: Holt, Rinehart and Winston; Renewed 1996; First Published: 1967; First Board Book Edition Published: 1996).

[2] Blake K. Healy, *The Veil: An Invitation to the Unseen Realm* (Lake Mary, FL: Charisma House Book Group, 2012).

reading about his life experiences provides a deeper understanding of the importance of identifying and encouraging the development of spiritual gifts in every child.

Samuel and the Auditory Learning Style

In God's initial visit with Samuel, God called Samuel's name. Samuel, with insight from Eli, eventually recognized that he was hearing the voice of God. God continued speaking, and Samuel heard many revelations directly from the mouth of God. Other notable scriptures that reference hearing include:

> He that hath an ear, let him hear what the Spirit saith unto the churches.
>
> Revelation 2:7. KJV

> Faith comes by hearing, and hearing by the word of God.
>
> Romans 10:17

> My own sheep will hear my voice and I know each one, and they will follow me.
>
> John 10:27, TPT

Polar Bear, Polar Bear, What Do You Hear?[1] is a children's book focusing on sound and hearing. It is another book written by Bill Martin, Jr. and illustrated by Eric Carle. Written specifically for children ages two to four years, rhythmical text repeatedly asks children what sounds they hear from a many animals.

Set in the zoo, the tumult of sounds include a growling polar bear, roaring lion, snorting hippopotamus, fluting flamingo, braying zebra, hissing boa constrictor, trumpeting elephant, snarling leopard, yelping peacock, and bellowing

---

[1] Bill Martin, Jr., *Polar Bear, Polar Bear, What Do You Hear?* (New York, NY: Henry Holt and Company, First Published: 1991, First Board Book Published: 1997).

walrus as well as the zookeeper. Listening activities for this book might include hearing audio of the sounds made by the animals in the book. Children usually take great delight in pretending to be animals, making animal sounds and repeating the words of the book over and over again as they read along.

Expanded learning might include an invented game similar to the one for visual learning. This time, after saying a child's name, ask the child, *What do you hear?* Again, variations to the game are unlimited and can be adapted to a variety settings and participants. An auditory game assists with the development of listening skills, environmental awareness, creativity, observation, taking turns and finding out what the child is hearing. Listening skills become important for children as they move into more formal academic experiences.

David and the Kinesthetic/Tactile Learning Style
King David was action oriented and "danced before the Lord with all his might" (2 Samuel 6:14). Miriam, Moses and Aaron's sister, was also a prophetess that danced joyfully.

> The prophetess, Miriam, Aaron's sister, picked up a tambourine, and all the rest of the women followed her with tambourines and joyful dancing.
> Exodus 15:20, Voice

Giraffes Can't Dance[1] by Giles Andrede and Guy Parker-Rees is a book filled with activity and movement.

The story is about Gerald the giraffe who wants to go to the annual jungle dance, but he has crooked knees and legs so thin they get tangled when he tries to dance. The other animals laugh just thinking about Gerald trying to dance. Gerald is sad and discouraged. A cricket encourages him to dance "to his own

---

[1] Giles Andrede and Guy Parker-Rees, *Giraffes Can't Dance* (New York, NY: Cartwheel Books, a division of Scholastic, Inc., Boardbook edition; March 1, 2012.

music." Gerald eventually discovers that he can dance his own special dance. Set in Africa, this lively story offers opportunities to learn about jungle animals, rhythmical movement and a variety of dances.

Expanded learning might include using a globe or map to find Africa and other interesting locations. The book can also prompt a conversation about emotions and the feelings experienced by the giraffe. Children usually need guidance as they learn to use words to identify and describe what they are feeling. Children cannot use their words until they have been taught what words to use, and when it is appropriate to use them.

Other expanded activities might include exploring movement of all kinds using a variety of musical sounds and styles. Offering opportunities for slow, graceful movement with waltzes as well as fast upbeat tempos allows children the opportunity to learn how to sync their movement with the music. Rhythm band instruments offer a fun way for active learners to channel their energy by banging drumsticks, shaking tambourines or playing whatever instrument they have. Moving to music in a variety of different ways using worship tools like flags and banners can be meaningful and fun for all ages. Everyone, adults and children, can get up, turn on the music and enjoy moving!

CHAPTER 4

Tools of Nurturing Books and Activities

Children's Books With Spiritual Applications

The children's books already discussed can be used to facilitate development of visual, auditory and kinesthetic/tactile learning styles. Many other children's books facilitate development of emerging language, literacy and prophecy skills. The idea is that if children have opportunities for learning with books when they are young, their caregivers can expand on that learning later at an opportune time to include more developmentally mature concepts and skills. The following books are a small sample of books with spiritual applications that caregivers can use for teachable moments as the Spirit leads.

The Very Hungry Caterpillar

The Very Hungry Caterpillar[1] was written and illustrated by Eric Carle. The story begins with a little egg on a leaf in the moonlight. The egg becomes a caterpillar that eats and eats and eats a variety of foods before forming a cocoon and finally emerging as a butterfly. The book uses a unique style that features distinct "eaten" holes on the pages and simple text with educational themes like counting numbers, naming the days of the week, identifying a variety of foods, and the life stages of a

---

[1] Eric Carle, *The Very Hungry Caterpillar* (Philomel Books, a division of Penguin Young Readers Group, First Board Book Edition 1994).

butterfly. Like other books by Eric Carle, the reader is introduced to basic science concepts; for example, the stages of metamorphosis are presented in this book.

Metamorphosis or transformation is a biblical principal taught in Romans.

> Do not allow this world to mold you in its own image. Instead, be transformed from the inside out by renewing your mind. As a result, you will be able to discern what God wills and whatever God finds good, pleasing, and complete.
>
> Romans 12:2, Voice

Another translation says:

> Stop imitating the ideals and opinions of the culture around you, but be inwardly transformed by the Holy Spirit through a total reformation of how you think. This will empower you to discern God's will as you live a beautiful life, satisfying and perfect in his eyes.
>
> Romans 12:2, TPT

This is a life verse for many believers. Revelation from this passage can continue to unfold throughout one's lifetime. Children who learn the foundational concept of metamorphosis early can apply that understanding to their own lives as they grow and mature.

The fruit of the spirit is another biblical study that can be introduced to children after reading *The Very Hungry Caterpillar.* In the story, the caterpillar eats a variety of fruit and other foods. Children need opportunities to explore all kinds of flavors (Psalm 34:8) using all their senses: taste, touch, smell, sight and sound. Expanded learning might include suggesting children listen to the sound of celery or carrots as they crunch down and take a bite. They can also learn about different food groups. This can be done by providing opportunities to experience a wide variety of vegetables and fruits. Take cantaloupe, for example. Explore it together using questions like: How does it feel, on the outside and on the inside? How does it smell? What color is it before it is cut open and what color is it on the inside? How does it taste? How does it compare to other melons like watermelon and honeydew?

Children can learn about fruits, vegetables and other foods. They can also learn about the fruit of the spirit. Children can be taught to practice and demonstrate spiritual fruit.

> But the fruit produced by Holy Spirit within you
> is divine love in all its varied expressions:
>> joy that overflows,
>> peace that subdues,
>> patience that endures,
>> kindness in action,
>> a life full of virtue,
>> faith that prevails,
>> gentleness of heart, and
>> strength of spirit.
> Never set the law above these qualities, for they
> are meant to be limitless.
>> Galatians 5:22-23, TPT

All children should be taught about kindness and gentleness. Caregivers can help children gain understanding by verbally labeling acts of kindness and gentleness. Opportunities for interacting with pets and new siblings is a great time for young children to learn about the fruit of the spirit. Holding and petting a new puppy might provide the perfect teachable moment for demonstrating kindness and gentleness. Other fruit of the spirit can be taught and demonstrated as the child matures and Holy Spirit leads.

Llama, Llama, Red Pajama

Llama, Llama, Red Pajama[1] by Anna Dewdny is one of a series of stories about Baby Llama and his mama. After a good-night kiss, Mama Llama tucks baby in bed, turns off the light and closes the bedroom door. Very quickly Baby Llama yells out asking for a drink and starts worrying when Mama does not bring the water immediately. Soft whimpers turn to hollers while Llama is waiting, waiting and waiting for his mama. Since Mama is not coming fast enough, Baby Llama starts to fret. In this rhythmical, rhyming read-aloud, Baby Llama turns bedtime into a full-blown llama drama! As the story ends, Mama Llama reassures Baby that she is near, will come as quickly as she can and always loves him even if he cannot see her. Mama kisses Baby again, and he falls peacefully asleep.

This book can provide a framework for helping children learn self-soothing, self-regulation and delay of gratification. It can be the catalyst for family discussions about topics like worry, trust and patience. At bedtime, preschoolers often need reassurance that they have not been left alone, their caregiver is nearby, they are loved and that they are capable of waiting with quiet confidence for their caregiver to be visibly present again.

Parents also need reassurance. At times, they may need to be reminded that they are loved by Father God. He will not leave them alone, and He will guide them by His Spirit when they do not know what to do. These Scriptures can provide reassurance that God is near; He is trustworthy, and His love is unending.

Trust

> Trust in the Lord completely, and do not rely on your own opinions. With all your heart rely on him to guide you, and he will lead you in every decision you make.

---

[1] Anna Dewdny, *Llama, Llama, Red Pajama* (New York, NY: Viking, an Imprint of Penguin Young Readers Group; 2005, 2015).

Proverbs 3:5, TPT

Worry

> Don't be pulled in different directions or worried about a thing. Be saturated in prayer throughout each day, offering your faith-filled requests before God with overflowing gratitude. Tell him every detail of your life, then God's wonderful peace that transcends human understanding, will make the answers known to you through Jesus Christ.
>
> Philippians 4:6-7, TPT

Never Abandoned

> You always have God's presence. For hasn't he promised you, "I will never leave you alone, never! And I will not loosen my grip on your life!"
>
> Hebrews 13:5, TPT

Every parent and child can experience feelings of being overwhelmed, isolated and discouraged. Much can be learned from the biblical example of David. When everything seemed to be going against him, Scripture tells us that he encouraged himself in the Lord (1 Samuel 30:6). One way that David overcame fear and negativity was to quiet and calm himself in the Presence of the Lord. As expressed in Psalm 131, David pictures the quiet rest of a child sitting on mother's lap.

> I am humbled and quieted in your presence. Like a contented child who rests on its mother's lap, I'm your resting child and my soul is content in you. O people of God, your time has come to quietly trust, waiting upon the Lord now and forever.

Psalm 131:2-3, TPT

Parents that gently and patiently help distressed children express their fears and then provide the needed comfort can teach their children how to calm themselves and move forward with courage. When parents calmly model a gentle quiet spirit (1 Peter 3:4), children can eventually learn to quiet themselves.

The Kissing Hand

The Kissing Hand[1] was written for children that are reluctant to go to school for the first time. Authored by Audrey Penn and illustrated by Ruth E. Harper and Nancy M. Leak, it is not available as a board book, because it has more text than picture books and is written specifically for older preschoolers.

As the story goes, school is starting in the forest and Chester Raccoon does not want to go. To help ease Chester's fears, Mrs. Raccoon shares a family secret called the kissing hand. Mrs. Raccoon kissed the palm of Chester's hand and told him that anytime he misses her or feels scared, he can press his hand to his cheek and be reassured of her love for him.

After reading the book, parents can share the kissing hand ritual with their children and explain to them that the kiss is a symbol of the parent's love. Stickers that are included at the back of the book can serve as reminders to children about their own kissing hands and the blessing of love that is demonstrated each time they press their hand to their cheek.

This story can prepare children for the first day of school, but it is also appropriate for other times of separation. It has been used to maintain a connection with a caregiver that is deployed and can be particularly meaningful when paired with video conferencing. If a child or family member has an extended hospital stay or a separation for any other reason, this book can be a significant reminder of the loving relationship.

Just as *The Kissing Hand* can be a reminder of caring

---

[1] Audrey Penn, *The Kissing Hand,* (Indianapolis, IN: Tanglewood Publishing, Inc., 2006).

human relationships, it can also be a reminder of an ever present and loving relationship with Almighty God. Many scriptural references apply including these two.

> Be strong and courageous. Do not be afraid or terrified because of them, for the LORD your God goes with you; he will never leave you nor forsake you.
>
> Deuteronomy 31:6, NIV

> The LORD appeared to us in the past, saying: "I have loved you with an everlasting love; I have drawn you with unfailing kindness.
>
> Jeremiah 31:3, NIV

The book can also serve to teach children about prophetic acts. A prophetic act is an action inspired by Holy Spirit that is a symbolic sign creating a connection between Earth and Heaven. Prophetic acts are demonstrated throughout the Bible. An example of a prophetic act is Moses holding his rod over the Red Sea, and the water dividing to make a path for the people to cross over and move forward.

> Raise your staff and stretch out your hand over the sea to divide the water so that the Israelites can go through the sea on dry ground.
>
> Exodus 14:16, NIV

One of the most notable prophetic acts is described in Exodus 12 when God instructed Hebrew families to kill a lamb and put its blood on the doorposts of their houses. At Passover, the death Angel passed over all the households protected by the blood of the lamb, and everyone inside the house was kept safe. Perhaps the most beloved memorial act is the sacrament of communion that was established by Lord Jesus Himself.

As children mature spiritually, it is important for them to develop an understanding of the importance of physical acts that have spiritual significance. The ritual of the kissing hand as described in this children's book is a simple example that can provide a foundation to build on for learning more about the meaning of prophetic acts later in the child's development.

On the Night You Were Born

On the Night You Were Born[1] is part of the *You Are Loved Collection* of children's books authored and beautifully illustrated by Nancy Tillman. The focus of this book is that of a joyous celebration for the birth and life of each child. It honors the uniqueness of every baby. The author describes a baby's birth as a delight that resonates throughout creation. Polar bears dance. The moon stays up all night. Even the trumpets in heaven are sounded in response to the baby's birth.

The theme of another book in the collection, *Wherever You Are: My Love Will Find You*,[2] is that of unstoppable, inescapable, unconditional love for the baby. The message of this celebratory picture book is one of joy and thanksgiving. Reading it out loud to a child is a way of declaring that the child is loved, accepted and wanted. All children need to have words of blessing spoken over them. When read aloud, the words in this book declare love for the little one that fills the atmosphere with blessings reaching all the way from Earth up into Heaven.

Many times in the Scripture Father God declares His passionate love over His children. Psalm 139, which is described as King David's poetic song, is filled with God's personal blessings. Take a look at the first ten verses.

> Lord, you know everything there is to know about me.
> You perceive every movement of my heart and soul,

---

[1] Nancy Tillman, *On the Night You Were Born* (New York, NY: Feiwel and Friends; an Imprint of Macmillan, Board Book Edition 2010).
[2] Nancy Tillman, *Wherever You Are: My Love Will Find You* (New York, NY: Feiwel and Friends; an Imprint of Macmillan, Board Book, Edition 2010).

and you understand my every thought before it
    even enters my mind.
You are so intimately aware of me, Lord.
You read my heart like an open book
and you know all the words I'm about to speak
before I even start a sentence!
You know every step I will take before my
    journey even begins.
You've gone into my future to prepare the way,
and in kindness you follow behind me
to spare me from the harm of my past.
With your hand of love upon my life,
you impart a blessing to me
This is just too wonderful, deep, and
    incomprehensible!
Your understanding of me brings me wonder
    and strength.
Where could I go from your Spirit?
Where could I run and hide from your face?
If I go up to heaven, you're there!
If I go down to the realm of the dead, you're
    there too
If I fly with wings into the shining dawn, you're
    there!
If I fly into the radiant sunset, you're there
    waiting
Wherever I go, your hand will guide me; your
    strength will empower me.
Psalm 139:1-10, TPT

The Lord is also described as a God Who rejoices over and
delights in His children. The Mighty Warrior God celebrates the
love He has for His people with great joy!

The LORD your God is with you,
    the Mighty Warrior who saves.
He will take great delight in you;

in his love he will no longer rebuke you,
but will rejoice over you with singing.
Zephaniah 3:17, NIV

The Living Bible expresses it like this, "Is that a joyous choir I hear? No, it is the Lord himself exulting over you in happy song." What an amazing Scripture! Father God Himself delights in and rejoices over His children. He even sings over His loved ones. What a great example for earthly parents!

God truly wants parents as well as their children to know they are loved and blessed. He also wants parents to share love and blessing with their children. God said it like this.

"I know the plans I have for you," declares the
LORD, "plans to prosper you and not to harm
you, plans to give you hope and a future."
Jeremiah 29:11, NIV

All parents need to personally know and experience the declarations and promises that are released in these faith-filled words. All children need someone to release these declarations and promises of a hopeful and prosperous future over them. In His mighty wisdom, Father has gifted every parent with the ability to decree and declare blessings over their children!

A Word to Grandparents and Other Caregivers

Grandparents and other caregivers often play an extraordinary and treasured role in the lives of young children. That role can include meaningful interactions with children, books and other literacy materials. Sharing time with little ones can be a blessing to both adult and child. Videoconferencing can make it possible for grandparents to read stories to their young grandchildren even if they live a great distance apart.

Books that are appropriate for a child's age and interest level make memorable gifts. When giving a book, always pray, decree and declare blessings over the recipient. In that way, every gift can become an anointed prayer cloth (Acts 19:12).

Gifts that are books can be an additional blessing if the giver and receiver share time together reading them.

Games, Activities, Experiences and Exploration

Emerging language, literacy and prophecy can be supported by expanded learning activities along with shared book reading. Perhaps one of the simplest and most effective activities that was previously described is the made-up game that follows this pattern: *(Name), (Name), what do you see, hear, feel, smell or taste?* This family game can be played at almost any age with any number of people in a wide variety of settings. Initially, the focus will be on identifying objects and vocabulary expansion. It can also provide opportunities for the development of environmental awareness and observational skills that are vital as children grow up in a world environment that seems to be increasingly challenging.

The same game can be played to activate and practice spiritual skills. The family should be the safest place for preparation, training and making corrections of spiritual skills. Giving children ongoing opportunities to share what they see, hear, smell, feel and taste can help them develop discernment, wisdom, knowledge and other prophetic skills. Children with the visual gift of seeing into the spirit realm can verbalize what they are seeing. Parents can provide support by giving them context, explanations and understanding. As parents listen and observe their children, they may begin to identify their children's gifts. The game can even be played like this: *Prophet, Prophet, what do you see?*

Safety

Safety issues should always be considered before beginning any activity with young children. They are naturally curious, always exploring and still have much to learn. Adults should plan ahead and provide protection from any potential safety concerns. Give children simple, understandable instructions that establish clear boundaries. Learning to follow directions is foundational for preparing children to transition to formal educational settings.

Caution:

- Follow all directives given by medical providers for each individual child and each age group.
- Children need adult supervision. Do not leave active, busy children alone.
- Read the child's cues and follow the child's lead in terms of recognizing when they are tired or not feeling well. No matter how special the activity, sometimes children just need to rest.
- Be aware of potential hazards. Considerations should include awareness of common allergies, water dangers and choking hazards.

See the sample resource list for safety concerns in the Appendix B. Many other safety resources are available to parents both in the community and online.

Ideas for Expanded Learning Activities

Some expanded learning suggestions for preschoolers are listed below. Activities can often be adapted for other ages and for the interests and preferences of each individual child. Hopefully, this list sparks new creative ideas that are initiated by both children and adults. The possibilities are unlimited.

- Let your child use a small flashlight to track the words of a book. Ask the child to shine the light on specific words and pictures. Children usually enjoy simple machines. If the child asks how the flashlight works, take it apart and explain. Be sure to include safety cautions.
- As a pre-cutting activity to strengthen the hand grip, let your child play with a paper punch. Use a shirt box to keep all materials together. Create pictures with paper, glue and the cut-out pieces.

- Play with playdough. Teach children not to eat playdough. (Caution: See information about choking hazards in the Appendix A.) Use tools like cookie cutters, miniature rolling pins and plastic knives. Structure the activity by keeping materials on a cookie sheet or plastic tablecloth. For language development ask, "How does it feel and smell?" and say, "Tell me about your creation."

- Go outside and blow bubbles together. The smallest bottles of bubbles are easier for little fingers to hold and can be easily refilled when empty. Ask, "What do you see, hear, smell?"

- Finger paint using shaving cream. Before beginning this activity, give children clear instructions, establish definite boundaries. Examples might include shaving cream must stay on the table; do not throw shaving cream; do not eat shaving cream. To protect children's clothing, they can wear an old adult shirt putting it on backwards.

- Listen to all kinds of music. Help the child develop an awareness of different sounds, rhythms and beats. Sing together. Dance together. Wave flags and banners. Move!

- Make or buy rhythm band instruments like bells, drum, tambourine or triangle. Move with the sounds. Take turns with the instruments. With more than one child, use a timer or change the music to let children know when it is time to switch instruments.
Again, establish simple rules before beginning the activity. The instruments can go in time-out if boundaries are violated.

- Make simple books using stickers or pictures glued to paper. Write simple text, e.g. *"I see the dog. The dog can run."* Be creative with the book style and materials used. Possibilities for cover pages might include paper from old wallpaper books and left-over wrapping paper. Use repetition like: *"I see the dog. I see the cat. I see Mom. I see Dad."* Use rhyme like:

> *I see the cat.*
> *I see the bat.*
> *I see the hat.*
> *I see the rat.*

- Go on a field trip to the park, fishing hole, zoo, aquarium, back yard or wherever. Explore together. Begin by establishing clear, concise safety rules. Have the child stop and take time to listen, smell, see. When appropriate, taste and touch. For vocabulary expansion, label and identify unknown animals and objects. Afterwards, let the child tell, dictate or write a story, and draw illustrations about the adventure.

- Go on a scavenger hunt. Make a simple written list of things to find like a rock, leaf, acorn, etc.

- Explore new foods or cook together. Let children feel and smell fruits like kiwi, plums and pineapple before cutting them open. Talk about colors, shapes and textures. Encourage tasting rather than requiring it. When learning about colors, provide a red, yellow and green apple. Do a taste test and let each person choose the one they think tastes the best. Cut apples in half horizontally. Notice the star shape inside. Find the seeds and talk about the life cycle of an apple growing from seed to tree to blossom to fruit. Ask open-ended questions. Listen to what the child has to say and answer their questions. (Caution: Food like uncut grapes, hot dogs, peanut butter and many others can be choking hazards. For further information about choking prevention and potential choking hazards see resources in the Appendix.)

- Count objects. Count in more than one language, e.g. uno, dos, tres. Teach counting in sign language.

- Make counting books using stickers, pictures or other objects. Start with 1, 2 and 3. On each page write a numeral, the corresponding written word, and the correct number of stickers or pictures. Let the child read the book; one, two, three! As children are ready, create more books with additional numbers adding a few at a time.

- Share, read or tell a story. Include siblings, parents and other caregivers. Take turns.
- Let your child tell a story. Write down your child's words. Ask the child to illustrate the story.
- After an activity, ask *What was your favorite thing? Was there anything you'd like to change?*
- Establish a bedtime routine. As part of your routine ask, *What was your favorite thing about today?* Share prayers together. Bless your child by speaking words of blessing!

Book Sharing Tips

After meeting basic needs, one of the most important gifts a parent or caregiver can give a child is to share books and read aloud to them. Book sharing encourages children to enjoy reading and supports early language and literacy development. An added benefit is the interaction between parent and child. Developing a positive relationship between children and their caregivers establishes the foundation for all the relationships children form in the future as they grow into adulthood and throughout life.[1]

A few tips, suggestions and reminders for sharing books with children are listed here:

- Read to your child every day. Make it your special time together even if it is only for a few minutes.
- Make the story come alive using dramatic expression and gestures. Change voices for different characters.

---

[1] American Academy of Pediatrics, Healthy Children.org, *Tips to Help Your Child Enjoy Reading Aloud*, https://www.healthychildren.org/English/ages-stages/gradeschool/school/Pages/Help-Your-Child-Enjoy-Reading-Aloud-Tips-for-Parents.aspx. Accessed 9/15/2019.

Act out or sing scenes or events from some books. Activate your theatrical talents.

- If your child loses interest, you don't have to finish a story.
- Observe and listen to your child's cues. Explore books by following your child's lead.
- Let your child choose the book even if it means reading the same book over and over. Repetition is foundational for early learning.
- Invite your child to read to you from a familiar book that is well known from having heard it so often.
- Ask about the illustrations in books; encourage your child to "read the pictures."
- Ask your child what will happen next.
- Read from a variety of children's books, including fairy tales, poetry, and nursery rhymes and a children's version of the Bible.
- Follow your child's interests when choosing the books. Many excellent books are available on non-fiction subjects such as the ocean, dogs, trucks, dinosaurs, butterflies, to name a few.
- Visit the children's section of your local library or bookstore.
- Reading should be fun for you and your child!

CHAPTER 5

Final Thoughts About Nurturing

Final Thoughts About Caregiving

Remember! Be fully present with your child during book sharing time and other activities. Often caregivers that are worn out and overwhelmed get energized and rejuvenated when they take time to enjoy their children.

Know your child. Read your child's cues and follow your child's lead. Learning, growth and development are all a process. Think about the emerging butterfly, the chick that is hatching, and the rose that is blossoming. Process takes time and patience.

Scriptures are filled with wisdom. Wisdom speaks about Creator God and His Creation. Wisdom has this to say about Father God's children.

> I laughed and played,
> so happy with what He made,
> while finding my delight
> in the children of men.
>
> Proverbs 8:31, TPT

Wisdom laughs and plays and delights in the children of men! Wisdom, the God kind of wisdom, teaches that happiness is found in valuing and enjoying the children; in laughing, playing and delighting with children. Remember that developing relationship is the key; it's foundational! Take time to play and have fun! Celebrate the joy of relationship!

Your Destiny

As a caregiver, there's so much to get done. Many details must be handled. Some things may seem repetitive, routine and even boring. Some things require urgent attention. Either way, it's easy for most of us to become so focused on the daily demands of caregiving that we lose sight of ourselves as a person. Sometimes we feel like just getting through the day is an accomplishment, and, as the days go by, we begin to feel like we've lost our own identity in the process.

Or maybe as we progress through our own lifespan into middle age and become senior adults, caregiving changes. Our days of caring for children at home are over. Some of us never had a family of our own, and we feel like it is too late now. We may begin to feel like we missed our opportunity, and there's no real future for us.

Whatever your circumstances, when feelings of disappointment, discouragement, depression and even hope deferred come knocking, what do you do? How do you prevent those feelings from taking root and becoming established? How do you encourage yourself in the Lord (1 Samuel 30:6) like David did when he lost everything at Ziklag? Do you have a comeback battle plan?

Here are some strategies you can prepare and practice so you become ready for any attack that may come against your body, mind, will and emotions.

One way to encourage yourself is to remember your personal heroes and heroes of the faith. These folks may or may not be famous. They may or may not be people you have personally met. The important thing is that they are individuals that positively and profoundly impacted you in some way. Make a list of your personal heroes and remember the special way each one touched you. Here are a few that are on my list.

- Victor Frankl was a survivor of the horrors of the Nazi death camps. His book, *Man's Search for Meaning,* is, in part, a chronicle of what he suffered and learned from that experience. One famous quote is, "Everything can be taken from a man but one thing: the last of the human freedoms; to choose one's attitude in any given set of circumstances, to choose one's own way."[1] His life and writings touch me deeply. No matter what I'm going through, his words encourage me to keep going, focus on moving forward and finish the challenge.

- Elsie Egermeier wrote *Egermeier's Bible Story Book.*[2] Elsie and my grandmother were cousins so both contributed to my spiritual DNA and the blessing of my Christian heritage. Dave and I, like many children of our generation, grew up hearing Elsie's stories. She was born in 1890 and as a teenager became interested in writing. At a time when most women did not work outside the home, she felt called by God to move to another state and write Christian books for children. She is described as having a great love for children, and it is said that she read her writings to children to be sure they understood and enjoyed the stories.[3] Writing Christian books that were

---

[1] Victor E. Frankl, *Man's Search for Meaning* (New York, NY: The Touchstone Edition, Simon and Shuster, Inc., 1984) 75

[2] Elsie E. Egermeier, *Egermeier's Bible Story Book* (Anderson, IN: Warner Press, 1923).

[3] Goodreads, *Elsie Egermeier,* https://www.goodreads.com/author/show/3887423.Elsie_Egermeier. Accessed 9/15/2019.

specifically for children was an innovative idea. Elsie was a pioneer whose books sold millions of copies and whose writings touched millions of lives.

- Max Brewer, my father, will always be a personal hero of mine. His life has been characterized by hard work, honesty and integrity. He worked long, physically demanding hours to provide for us. Many days he must have been tired, even exhausted, but he always took time to be caring, kind and nurturing. A humble man, he would be quite surprised to be thought of as a hero of faith. In the midst of the busyness of life, he would take time to be sure we saw God's glory in the world around us. He made sure we experienced the sunrise, rainbows and all the phases of moonlight. For eternity, I will be grateful for my father and the gentle way he cared for us and shared his great love for the beauty of nature. The love my earthly father demonstrated every day has helped me know and receive the eternal love of my heavenly Father.

Another strategy you can use to encourage yourself is knowing the Word of God. We live in an amazing time when we have unlimited access to the Bible. It is available anytime, anywhere in multiple translations. Knowing the Word can mean reading, studying, meditating, learning, memorizing and even saturating yourself in it. The Bible is alive! Spend time with it. It has the power to activate spirits, increase faith and transform us.

So here's what I want you to do, God

helping you: Take your everyday, ordinary life—your sleeping, eating, going-to-work, and walking-around life—and place it before God as an offering. Embracing what God does for you is the best thing you can do for him. Don't become so well-adjusted to your culture that you fit into it without even thinking. Instead, fix your attention on God. You'll be changed from the inside out. Readily recognize what he wants from you, and quickly respond to it. Unlike the culture around you, always dragging you down to its level of immaturity, God brings the best out of you, develops well-formed maturity in you.

Romans 12:1-2, MSG

Notice the phrase "changed from the inside out." The New Living Translation is clear in making that point.

Don't copy the behavior and customs of this world, but let God transform you into a new person by changing the way you think. Then you will learn to know God's will for you, which is good and pleasing and perfect.

That is encouraging! We can change and be transformed. Metamorphosis is available as we align our thinking with God's Word. It's important to make a list of foundational life verses that are especially meaningful to you. Whenever you face challenging circumstances, remember those life verses and hold them close. If you feel overwhelmed, search for what the Bible says about that specific situation and anchor your faith to that Word.

Fellowship is also an excellent way to encourage yourself. Spending time with caring family and friends can be very encouraging. Just being surrounded by people who love you and will support you, even when you are wrong, can be very encouraging. Isolation and feeling alone can quickly result in a downward spiral. Take time develop to relationships with people of precious, like-minded faith.

It's even more important to take time to develop relationship with the Lord Jesus and know the value of that relationship.

> The priceless privilege (the overwhelming preciousness, the surpassing worth, and supreme advantage) of knowing Christ Jesus my Lord and of progressively becoming more deeply and intimately acquainted with Him [of perceiving and recognizing and understanding Him more fully and clearly].
> Philippians 3:8, AMPC

To know Him is to know that He loves you with an everlasting love (Jeremiah 31:3). He has great future planned for you. As He said,

> I know the plans I have for you," declares the LORD, "plans to prosper you and not to harm you, plans to give you hope and a future."
> Jeremiah 29:11, NIV

Spend some quality time getting to know Him. Worship, dance, sing, pray in the Spirit of God and pray with the understanding. Repent and ask for forgiveness when it is needed. Release forgiveness to others. Rejoice! Take communion. Commune with Him. As you quiet yourself, lean in and just listen.-You will come to know He loves you and has a great plan for you. He is more than able to restore hope and renew strength!

A Word of Thanks

Every time you cross my mind, I break out in

exclamations of thanks to God. Each exclamation is a trigger to prayer. I find myself praying for you with a glad heart.

Philippians 1:3, MSG

Recently, Father told me that He was well pleased with the caregivers in His Kingdom. He was talking about parents, grandparents, marriage partners, single parents, adoptive parents, grandparents raising grandchildren, foster parents, extended family members, children's ministers, babysitters, childcare workers, neighbors, professionals, senior volunteers, intercessors and all the others that provide care for children. He included all those that have laid down their lives, time, effort, money and prayers for the little ones, the innocents. All those that have made a choice to honor Father by helping to care for His children.

In a world system that has launched horrendous never-ending attacks against marriage, family and children, the caregivers have chosen life. He reminded me of this verse and said it describes all of you. "Choose today whom you will serve...as for me and my family, we will serve the LORD" (Joshua 24:15, NLT). Father is saying, "You have chosen His way. It is the most excellent way.'" (1 Corinthians 12:31, NIV). That is the way of love.

Directly from Father's heart, thank you to each and every caregiver. All your efforts have eternal consequences. Your work with children has made an impact that will result in benefits for all eternity. You are valued! You are appreciated! Thank you!

DAVID AND KATHIE BURNETT

Appendix A

Resources for parent issues

The reader should note that this is not a comprehensive list of resources. Internet resources can quickly become outdated, may provide information that is unreliable or that is not based on current research. Websites are frequently taken down, removed or become unavailable. The reader is urged to use common sense and wisdom when accessing these resources. The reader is strongly encouraged to access additional resources, particularly with professionals available in the community.

Suicide Prevention Lifeline
- Call 1-800-273-8255
- Available 24 hours
- The Lifeline provides 24/7, free and confidential support for people in distress, prevention and crisis resources for you or your loved ones, and best practices for professionals.
- https://suicidepreventionlifeline.org

National Domestic Violence Hotline
- 1-800-799-7233
- 1-800-787-3224 TTY for deaf or hard of hearing; video phone at 1-855812-1001
- Highly trained expert advocates are available 24/7 to talk confidentially with anyone in the United States who is experiencing domestic violence, seeking resources or information, or questioning unhealthy aspects of their relationship.

- https://www.thehotline.org/help

National Sexual Assault Telephone Hotline–RAINN
- 800-656-4873
- Call 800.656.HOPE (4673) to be connected with a trained staff member from a sexual assault service provider in your area.
- https://www.rainn.org/about-national-sexual-assault-telephone-hotline

Substance Abuse and Mental Health Services Administration (SAMHSA) National Helpline
- 1-800-662-HELP (4357)
- SAMHSA's National Helpline is a free, confidential, 24/7, 365-day-a-year treatment referral and information service (in English and Spanish) for individuals and families facing mental and/or substance use disorders.
- https://www.samhsa.gov/find-help/national-helpline

National Drug Helpline
- 1-888-633-3239
- The National Drug Helpline offers 24/7 drug and alcohol help to those struggling with addiction. Call the national hotline for drug abuse today to receive information regarding treatment and recovery.
- http://drughelpline.org

Postpartum Support International (PSI) for Postpartum Depression
- 1-800-944-4773
- Text: 503-894-9453
- The PSI Helpline does not handle emergencies. People in crisis should call their local emergency number or the National Suicide Prevention Hotline at 1-800-273-TALK (8255).
- http://www.postpartum.net

Resources accessed December 2018

DAVID AND KATHIE BURNETT

Appendix B

Resources with information about childhood issues

The reader should note that this is not a comprehensive list of resources. Internet resources can quickly become outdated, may provide information that is unreliable or that is not based on current research. Websites are frequently taken down, removed or become unavailable. The reader is urged to use common sense and wisdom when accessing these resources. The reader is strongly encouraged to access additional resources, particularly medical professionals and other community resources.

Child development
American Academy of Pediatrics, Healthy Children. Org, Ages and Stages,
https://www.healthychildren.org/english/ages-stages/pages/default.aspx

General safety
Safe Kids Worldwide, a website that offers safety tips on many issues for a variety of ages,
https://www safekids.org/safetytips
The National Safety Council. https://www.nsc.org/home-safety

Allergies and asthma

American Academy of Allergy, Asthma and Immunology (AAAA), Prevention of Allergies and Asthma in Children,
https://www.aaaai.org/conditions-and-treatments/library/allergy-library/prevention-of-allergies-and-asthma-in-children

Baby's cues

March of Dimes; Learning Your Baby's Cues,
https://www.marchofdimes.org/complications/learning-your-baby-s-cues.aspx

Parenting; 11 Important Baby Cues Every Parent Needs to Know,
https://www.parenting.com/baby/11-important-baby-cues

Car seats

National Highway Traffic Safety Association (NHTSA), Car Seats and Booster Seats,
https://www.nhtsa.gov

Childproofing

https://www.childproofingexperts.com/childproofing-checklist-by-age

United States Consumer Product Safety Commission, Childproofing Your Home—12 Safety Devices to Protect Your Children,
https://www.cpsc.gov/safety-education/safety-guides/kids-and-babies/childproofing-your-home-12-safety-devices-protect

Kids' Health from Nemours, Child Health and Preventing Household Accidents,
Childproofing Experts.com, Childproofing Checklist by Age,
https://kidshealth.org/en/parents/childproof.html

Choking

Centers for Disease Control and Prevention (CDC), *Choking Hazards,*

https://www.cdc.gov/nutrition/infantandtoddlernutrition/foo
ds-and-drinks/choking-hazards.html

Crying
The Period of Purple Crying, http://purplecrying.info

*Mayo Clinic, Infant and Toddler Health, Crying Baby: What to Do when
Your Newborn Cries*,
https://www.mayoclinic.org/healthy-lifestyle/infant-and-
toddler-health/in-depth/healthy-baby/art-20043859

Drowning
Centers for Disease Control and Prevention (CDC), Drowning Prevention,
https://www.cdc.gov/safechild/drowning/index.html

Feeding
Centers for Disease Control and Prevention (CDC), Infant Feeding,
https://www.cdc.gov/healthywater/hygiene/healthychildcare/i
nfantfeeding.html

Poison
Poison Control hotline at 1-800-222-1222. Post in an easy to reach
location. Prevention tip:
https://www.webpoisoncontrol.org/?gclid=EAIaIQobChMIsp
WB_93F3wIVBLbACh2RAgTEEAAYAiAAEgLxVfD_BwE

Recalls
United States Consumer Product Safety Commission,
https://www.cpsc.gov/Recalls

Secondhand Smoke
Centers for Disease Control and Prevention (CDC), Secondhand Smoke (SHS)
https://www.cdc.gov/tobacco/data_statistics/fact_sheets/seco
ndhand_smoke/general_facts/index.htm

Self-Care
SCAN Parent Resource Center, Self-Care for Parents Tip Sheet in English
https://www.scanva.org/wp-
content/uploads/2013/06/SelfCare2016_English.pdf

SCAN Parent Resource Center, Self-Care for Parents Tip Sheet in Spanish, Cuidado personal para padres,
https://www.scanva.org/wpcontent/uploads/2013/06/SelfCar
e2016_Spanish.pdf

Sleep
American Academy of Pediatrics, Safe Sleep
https://www.aap.org/en-us/advocacy-and-policy/aap-health-
initiatives/healthy-child-care/Pages/Safe-Sleep.aspx

March of Dimes Safe Sleep for Your Baby,
https://www.marchofdimes.org/baby/safe-sleep-for-your-
baby.aspx

How to Keep Your Sleeping Baby Safe: AAP Policy Explained, Healthy Children
https://www.healthychildren.org/English/ages-
stages/baby/sleep/Pages/A-Parents-Guide-to-Safe-Sleep.aspx

National Institute for Child Health and Human Development (NICHD), Safe to Sleep, https://safetosleep.nichd.nih.gov

Sudden Infant Death Syndrome (SIDS)

Mayo Clinic, Sudden Infant Death Syndrome (SIDS), https://www.mayoclinic.org/diseases-conditions/sudden-infant-death-syndrome/symptoms-causes/syc-20352800

American SIDS Institute, Reduce the Risk, https://sids.org/what-is-sidssuid/reduce-the-risk

National Sleep Foundation, Sudden Infant Death Syndrome and Sleep https://www.sleepfoundation.org/sleep-disorders-problems/sudden-infant-death-syndrome-and-sleep

Resources accessed December 2018

DAVID AND KATHIE BURNETT

PART THREE

Authors Pages

Our Testimony

Prayer of Blessings and Decrees for the Reader

About the Authors

Our Testimony

Kathie

> The hand of the LORD was on me, and he brought me out by the Spirit of the LORD and set me in the middle of a valley; it was full of bones. He led me back and forth among them, and I saw a great many bones on the floor of the valley, bones that were very dry. He asked me, "Son of man, can these bones live?"
>
> I said, "Sovereign LORD, you alone know."
>
> Then he said to me, "Prophesy to these bones and say to them, 'Dry bones, hear the word of the LORD! This is what the Sovereign LORD says to these bones: I will make breath enter you, and you will come to life. I will attach tendons to you and make flesh come upon you and cover you with skin; I will put breath in you, and you will come to life. Then you will know that I am the LORD.'" So I prophesied as I was commanded.
>
> Ezekiel 37:1-7, NIV

Ezekiel 37 was the passage I heard Chuck Pierce minister on a Friday during a Dutch Sheets' conference. The following morning, I woke up around 5 a.m. thinking we needed to study that passage again. As I grabbed the iPad, Dave made a strange noise. I quickly realized he was experiencing the violent shaking of a grand mal seizure. That had never happened before! After the seizure, Dave was unresponsive. He was locked in a fetal position with his hands tightly curled. His breathing was labored. He gurgled and struggled with every breath. He was totally unresponsive. Holy Spirit immediately let me know we were going to "do" (activate) Ezekiel 37, not study it! I said, "Father, You know!" I cried, "Jesus! I speak life!" Over and over, "Jesus! I speak life." "Jesus! I speak life." "Jesus! I speak life." Dave was still unresponsive.

I called 911. Three EMTs and at least three police officers responded to the call. They did their thing. Dave continued to be unresponsive. The lead EMT looked at his partner and shook his head back and forth as if to say, "This is not good." They both turned to me and with a grim look said, "We're taking him to the hospital."

At the hospital, he was immediately taken to get a CT scan. Later, he told me he "came to" in the "tube" during the scan. That was really a startling place for him to wake up! When Dave came out of the scan, he didn't remember anything that happened. But he was alert, fully oriented and able to communicate!

But God!!! Hallelujah!

Later, the neurologist told us that, based on the EMT's report, Dave had been unresponsive for at least 45 minutes. At the hospital, Dave had an MRI and an echocardiogram along with the CT scan. Test results revealed there was no evidence of a stroke or tumor. All tests were described as "clear!" After a couple of days, Dave was released from the hospital.

Although he has no diagnosis, he has experienced some major lifestyle changes. Immediately, Dave was required to stop driving for three months, per a state law in Texas. This was a type of fast that was challenging not only because Dave enjoys driving but also because it meant he had to ride with me. Since I tend to drive like a prophet (no offense intended to anyone!), that meant Dave really had to be "prayed up" everywhere we went!

Dave also felt led by Holy Spirit to fast social media. Since he had several thousand Facebook friends, this was a very meaningful fast for him. The 90 days he fasted driving, as required, and social media (as directed by Holy Spirit) became a time of intense intercession for him.

Dave was also put on a preventative medication that resulted in significant side effects. He continues to battle through each challenge. He works to strengthen himself both physically and spiritually. As the Word says, "Finally, my brethren, be strong in the Lord and in the power of His might" (Ephesians 6:10).

Dave

The Awakening
I woke up on the morning of June 16, 2018 in a CT Tube in Medical City Hospital in Denton, Texas. All I remember is that I went to sleep in our home in Corinth, Texas and woke up in the hospital in Denton. I have no recollection of anything that happened in between those times, but I am thankful that by the grace of God I woke up.

What I have since learned is that in the predawn hours of that Saturday morning, my wife Kathie discovered me in the midst of what would be diagnosed as a grand mal seizure. Kathie began to pray and speak life over me. She also called 911, which resulted in numerous emergency responders filling our home. Unable to bring me to consciousness, the EMTs decided to transport me to the hospital.

As I came out of the CT Tube, I seemed to be alert and conversationally coherent. Following a couple of days in the hospital, additional tests and consultation with a neurologist, no one could provide an explanation as to why the seizure occurred. The recovery of physical and mental stamina remains a work in progress.

I am so very grateful for the grace and love of God, for unfolding revelation from Holy Spirit and for the love and intercession of a wonderful Spirit-filled wife. Daily walking and the discipline of this writing project are key components of the process and pursuit to recover all (1 Samuel 30:8). What manifested on that Saturday morning in June as a physical awakening has emerged as an ongoing process of Spiritual revelation and awakening.

Together

Praise the Ancient of Days! Praise the great I Am! We are grateful!!! He is able to do above and beyond all we hope or imagine! The Amplified, says *He will.*

> "Do superabundantly more than all that we dare ask or think [infinitely beyond our greatest prayers, hopes, or dreams]."
>
> Ephesians 3:20, AMP

That same verse in the Passion Translation says,

> "Never doubt God's mighty power to work in you and accomplish all this. He will achieve infinitely more than your greatest request, your most unbelievable dream, and exceed your wildest imagination! He will outdo them all, for His miraculous power constantly energizes you."

Be encouraged! We are going beyond!

Prayers of Blessing for the Reader

Father God,

Thank you for each one that read this book! We believe that You determined this time in history as the appointed time for every reader to be alive on planet Earth (Acts 17:26). We believe that each one was born for such a time as this (Esther 4:14). We believe that everyone that has read the vision will be equipped and empowered to run with it (Habakkuk 2:2) and will be able to fully enter in to the tri-generational family blessing (Deuteronomy 6:7).

In Jesus' Name, we bless the readers and release faith for the following decrees and declarations to fully manifest in their lives and the lives of each member of their households, the young and old and the near and far!

We invite every reader to pray this declaration of faith to Father God:

> You keep every promise you've ever made to
> me!
> Since your love for me is constant and endless,
> I ask you, Lord, to finish every good thing that
> you've begun in me!
>
> Psalm 138:8, TPT

The following is our decree, declaration and prayer of faith for you:

I pray with great faith for you, because I'm fully convinced that the One who began this glorious work in you will faithfully continue the process of maturing you and will put his finishing touches to it until the unveiling of our Lord Jesus Christ!

Philippians 1:6, TPT

We decree and declare that you enter into the fullness of God's perfect plan for your life. It is written,
I know the plans I have for you," declares the LORD, "plans to prosper you and not to harm you, plans to give you hope and a future.

Jeremiah 29:11, NIV

We decree and declare you will know and experience the ongoing peace of God. It is written,
You will keep in perfect peace all who trust in you, all whose thoughts are fixed on you!

Isaiah 26:3, NLT

We decree and declare,
Trust in the Lord completely, and do not rely on your own opinions. With all your heart rely on him to guide you, and he will lead you in every decision you make.

Proverbs 3:5-6, TPT

We decree and declare you are able to rise above your circumstances to discern the wisdom of God because you are seated "with Him in the heavenly places in Christ Jesus" (Ephesians 2:6, KJV) and you will look and see,

> "A door standing open in heaven" and hear a voice say, "Come up here, and I will show you what must take place after this."
>
> Revelation 4:1, NIVS

We decree and declare, you are

> Strong in the Lord and in his mighty power.
>
> Ephesians 6:10, NIV

and

> The joy of the LORD is your strength.
>
> Nehemiah 8:10

We decree and declare that you are not worried or anxious but you will continuously

> Be cheerful with joyous celebration in every season of life. Let joy overflow, for you are united with the Anointed One! Let gentleness be seen in every relationship, for our Lord is ever near. Don't be pulled in different directions or worried about a thing. Be saturated in prayer throughout each day, offering your faith-filled requests before God with overflowing gratitude. Tell him every detail of your life, then God's wonderful peace that transcends human understanding, will make the answers known to you through Jesus Christ.
>
> Philippians 4:4-7, TPT

DAVID AND KATHIE BURNETT

About the Authors

David Burnett is a voice called to proclaim God's family plan for multigenerational blessing. As a reflection of Father's heart, he seeks to reconcile and realign generations to flow together in an anointing of love and honor. His vision is for the restoration of households as the foundation for thriving families, tribes and nations. Although he has experienced almost a half-century in ministry, it is in the experience of recovery from brokenness in his personal and family history that Holy Spirit is shaping and sending him in this season. Through writing, preaching, personal ministry and intercessory prayer, Dave is compelled to comfort others with the comfort with which God has graciously comforted him (2 Corinthians 1:4).

Kathie Jan Brewer Burnett is a fifth generation teacher that has used her gifts in the ministry as well as in both public and private schools. In the market place, she has served as a trainer, counselor, monitor and consultant in local, state and federal programs. She is a passionate lover of God's Word in all its various forms and translations believing that He is "sustaining all things by His powerful Word" (Hebrews 1:3, NIV).

Dave and Kathie's contact information:

Email: DTandKJBurnett@gmail.com

https://www.facebook.com/GodsFamilyPlan

Made in the USA
Lexington, KY
16 September 2019